The FATHER Style

Style

A fresh look
at the nature of
God the Father

GAYLE D. ERWIN

YAHSHUA
PUBLISHING

YAHSHUA Publishing
PO Box 219
Cathedral City, CA 92235-0219
Phone (619) 321-0077
Fax (619) 324-3006

Unless otherwise noted, all Scripture references are from the King James Version of the Bible.

Scripture references, where noted, are from the Holy Bible, New International Version, copyright 1973, 1978, by the New York International Bible Society. Used by permission of Zondervan Bible Publishers.

Table of Contents

Introduction

Many people see the Father as this white-haired old man sitting somewhere on a cosmic rock, very irritated and looking for some human being to zap. Then many people feel that Jesus comes along and says, "I know Dad has moods, so you stick with me and I will get things for you." This split view between Jesus and God the Father cannot be accurate.

When Jesus said, "When you see me you see the Father," and "I and the Father are one," he gave us a statement that should destroy all prior misconceptions. Unfortunately, misunderstanding still abounds.

I thought about this split thinking and wondered where we went wrong. Surely, the Father had been trying to indicate his nature to us in the Old Testament, but we managed to overlook that revelation. Surely, this nature of the Father would match that of Jesus. How did we miss it? With this thought in mind, I went back to the Old Testament (looking through the lens of the nature of Jesus) to verify my theory that God the Father revealed himself specifically to be the same in nature as Jesus.

If you wonder what that lens is like, I urge you to read first the opening pages of the section called "The Rock."

If you have read my prior book, **The Jesus Style**, then you are aware of that lens and the list of 14 points of the nature of Jesus. Even if you have not read the prior book, this book will stand on its on.

So, knowing that Jesus and the Father must be of the same essence, I searched and found the revealing events that verified the theory. That discovery continues to energize my life and strengthen my love for God.

Enough. Let us now join one of my favorite persons, Moses, in Exodus 3.

THE FATHER STYLE

Part One

THE DESERT

What Is Your Name?

I AM WHO I AM

Shoeless, hiding his face before the fire in a lowly thorn bush, Moses trembled at the charge given by the voice. How could he comprehend or respond?

"Tell the Israelites that I AM WHO I AM, the God of your fathers has sent you."

Moses knew that name—I AM. He knew that early in history mankind called upon God by that name. He also knew that God had first revealed himself by that name to Abraham when he called him to leave Ur of the Chaldees.

Moses, by special arrangement, roamed Pharaoh's courts and colleges before his assignment to free his kinsmen. Training and power aimed him toward the Egyptian monarchy until the two cultures that clashed within him collapsed every dream in his heart. The time seemed ripe in Moses' mind for his best self-energized effort to produce freedom and fulfill the highest calling in his breast as he slew an Egyptian to rescue an Israeli.

Instead, all he bought was *fleedom*. For forty lonely fugitive years he herded sheep he didn't own. Forty years! Forty years of the same path, same sheep, same "baaa." Forty years! What have you ever done for forty years so boring?

Perhaps, after forty years of this slow desert sameness, God said, "Now, I can talk to that man. Perhaps now he will listen to my mind and not his own." I have often prayed, "God, don't let me get so stubborn that it takes you forty years to talk to me."

Here, in the face of the consuming fire (or was it the *unconsuming fire*?) every dream he ever had returned, this time in living color. Now, sent by the I AM rather than himself, he was to return to the courts of Pharaoh as an enemy of the state but a deliverer of the children of God. The two cultures, Egyptian and Jewish, that clashed within him are now reduced to one.

"This is my name forever, the name by which I am to be remembered from generation to generation."

Now, God's name exceeded any passing adjectives. This "forever" revelation identified God even for us to this day in the name-giving encounter.

What is that Name Again?

This I AM WHO I AM is the name God *chose* for himself and not one I have given to him. Many of the Old Testament names used for God are good and give understanding about God, but most of them are simply descriptive names used by individuals as a result of their own experience of God or understanding of God.

The commonly used (though, as we will see, inaccurate) "Jehovah" is attached by hyphen to several descriptive Hebrew words and called "names" by many people. Jeremiah, in Chapter 33, called him "Jehovah is our righteousness." Ezekiel, in Chapter 48, called the heavenly Jerusalem "Jehovah is there." Gideon called an altar he built "Jehovah is peace." Moses named an altar in Exodus 17, "Jehovah is my banner." Abraham named the place where God rescued him from sacrificing Isaac "Jehovah will provide." David called him, "Jehovah my shepherd" in Psalms 23 and "Jehovah most high" in Psalm 7. Samuel tells us that Elkanah sacrificed annually to the "Jehovah of hosts."

Only two of these names come from the lips of God: Through Moses God declares himself to be "Jehovah who heals you" and "Jehovah who sanctifies you." So, most of the names we have used for God are experiential, and, though good and revealing, are not ones he has chosen for himself. I AM WHO I AM is his own chosen forever name.

This name has a central understanding as *self existent*, but along with it comes the understanding of absolute, undeceiving reality, a sense of honesty and openness. Had I been the one to send Moses, reality would have forced me to say "I ain't" has sent you or the "great maybe."

So much of my life (some of it taught by culture but most of it simply my carnal nature) is spent in deceptive forms. "Don't let anyone know your true feelings." "Keep a stiff upper lip." "Keep smiling." "Keep your cards hidden." "Keep it a secret."

The very name of God attached by his grace to our spirits calls us to a position of reality and honesty. His very name and nature is an invitation, a force to pull us from the hiding that marked the fall of Adam. Honesty is the call and goal of the Church, and any time we grovel in church secrecy, in hiding, in deceptive practices, we are fighting against the pull of God and shaming his name and our name. Every culture embodies deception in some form, but we are citizens of the kingdom of God whose king is "Light" and who has no darkness (thus no deception) in him. (1 John 1:5)

I AM as an eternal name raises a delightful side thought. Ephesians 3:14 reveals that his whole family in earth derives its name from him, thus our family name is I AM WHO I AM. Whatever last name or family name I had before must now have an addition that is stronger and more significant—I AM. I must understand that my name is now Gayle Erwin I AM as a member of *His* family. You must add I AM to your last name if you are to understand our family relationship. (See Naming the Family in Part Six.)

Tell Me How You Pronounce That

The name itself provides an additional source of insight. I AM WHO I AM is written in its English form, YHWH (sometimes called the tetragrammaton). Whatever the pronunciation, it could not be known from the writing because of the absence of vowels in the writing and, by the time vowels could be added, the pronunciation passed down verbally had been lost.

You are probably aware that in almost all versions of the Bible that are published, when you see the word "LORD" in the Old Testament, that is the word accepted as the translation for YHWH. In some translations it is written as all capitals. This is *not* the actual translation or transliteration or a sound-alike of the name. If this seems like a complaint from me, it is. My view of the validity of the Bible is pained when inaccuracies are deliberately introduced. So, when you see the word "LORD" capitalized like that in the Old Testament, in your mind peel it up and see "YHWH" under it.

Before Jesus, the spiritual leaders of Israel decreed that this sacred memorial name must not be spoken under penalty of death. This decree explains why listeners picked up stones to kill Jesus when he spoke the name in John 8. However, God never demanded silence on his name. Like any father, he wanted to be known by his children and especially to be *known* by that name. So strict had the traditions become, that when Jesus said "Abba" he broke all the rules.

If we were to demand *absolute* accuracy of our translations, then we would print YHWH rather than LORD (Orthodox Jews would be silent not attempting to pronounce YHWH). "Jehovah," as a name, appears to have few arguments going for it. As history goes, "Jehovah" has only been used for the past few centuries and apparently was the attempt by some to drop the vowels of "Adonai" another word for "Lord" into the unpronounceable YHWH and adjust it to the word "Jehovah."

Once again, if we demanded absolute accuracy of ourselves, we would probably never use the name "Jehovah." However, don't be dismayed at the thought that your prayers might be diverted or rejected by use of such an inaccurate name. Our God, who does all things well, hears our hearts and includes all our mistakes in the covering of his grace as we will see very well on later pages.

Although absolute proof is lacking, a good case can be made that the letters "YHWH" are pronounced as "Yahweh." The preservation of the first syllable "Yah" through the centuries is a rich vein of evidence. Whenever we say "Hal-lel-u-Yah" we are using that name. Different people's names have preserved it: Jeremi-Yah, Zechari-Yah, Eli-Yah. In Psalms 68:4, David tells us God rides on the clouds by his name YAH. So, the evidence is strong. My personal conclusion,which I share with you in the following paragraphs, recognizes both the grace of God and the authority of Scripture.

Which Name Should I Use?

The question naturally arises as we look at God's revelation of his name and the naming of his son, "Just which name is right and which one should I use?" God has honored our communication with him for centuries, whatever language or words naming deity we have used, because he knows our hearts.

When I am among the spiritually powerful Shona tribesmen of Africa, I hear them call God "Mwari." I know who they are talking about; they know who they are talking about; and I think YHWH God knows who they are talking about. The same case can be made for our English words or for the words of any language or culture. I believe there is a danger of taking grace only so far as to save us, then snapping back into legalism when it comes to names and languages.

The real understanding (I hope I will make this clear) is that God's nature is attached firmly to his name. *If we hit his name and miss his nature, we have violated him regardless of how smug we may feel about our accuracy.* My own name, Gayle Erwin, is routinely misspelled and mispronounced. Basically, I don't care about those misspellings as long as you don't misunderstand or misrepresent me. God is even more understanding and gracious—certainly more knowing. Indeed, Revelation 5:9 and 14:6 emphasize that he is the God of every nation, tribe and tongue and he gathers them to himself. So, I feel no need to *demand* the use of the Hebrew words or even to prohibit the use of the word "Jehovah."

Knowing both the surety of Scripture and the grace of God, I am comfortable in personal prayer and communication with God using the name "Yahweh." In communication with other people, I freely use the common term "Lord" as a replacement for "YHWH" for the sake of understanding. We are free to use the actual names, but I don't think God intended for divisions to come over that subject.

YHWH gave us that name to remember him. Let us not *forget*. That is the point. He wants us to talk to him.

What an awesome wall to be backed against—to have the most important name in eternity given to us and yet not be able to pronounce it or address it directly. Though we may choose comfortably to pronounce it "Yahweh", we lack absolute certainty. Some representative, more intimate with God than we, must come with a revelation. Against *that* wall one can only wail as he waits on another deliverer like Moses who can hear what the Father says.

Now that Moses knows the name of God, a power flow begins that will shake the earth's ruling kingdom, but an extremely important facet is missing. Though Moses is unaware, another encounter is coming which will be more eternity-shaking than the desert experience. Until then, his knowledge is inadequate.

Meanwhile, Back in the Tent

A few plagues later we rejoin Moses after the successful completion of his confrontation with the King of Egypt. He is now back in his familiar desert, but the conditions are completely different. Now, he is leading a band of newly-released slaves who seem intent on displaying the baser parts of their humanity. Awesome events have been experienced by the Children of Israel during their release from the hands of a hostile Pharaoh, including the Plagues of Egypt, the crossing of the Red Sea and the reception of the Law, but that did not deter them from a shameful and promiscuous romp around a golden calf they had crafted with their own hands and worshiped as their new god.

As we look in on Moses, he is in a tent, a special one called the "Tent of Meeting" built as a place to consult with God. This tent is not quite the *Tabernacle* yet, but it soon will be. His immediate goal is to keep the great YHWH, with whom he has a close relationship, from destroying this rebellious, idol worshiping slave-band and to persuade YHWH to continue to travel with them.

Moses succeeds. YHWH relents and offers him a most unusual opportunity. He informs

Moses, "I will do what you ask." Quick to sign another contract with this YHWH, Moses asks the question that will shake eternity and provide the very core of this book.

I Want to See You

And he said, I beseech thee, shew me
thy glory. Exodus 33:18

When the mouth cries "I want to see God," the heart has reached its finest moment. To *make our fortune* or to *make our own way* is admired as a fine goal in our culture. We honor those who have *made it* in life; but, if somehow we could know the truth early in our lives, we would erase all honor and ignore all fortune to search out the Glory of God. Once we have sought and seen God, all other necessary things have a way of coming to us. May God save us from the bondage of needing to *make it*.

When you love someone, you want to see them. Letters and phone calls are fine as far as they go, but love drives you to their presence. Moses obviously loved God—he wanted to see him.

Moses thought this encounter a mere argument which, once again, he had won, not knowing that in this moment he had pressed the edges of eternity and asked the question that would bring him to the crowning moment of his life. Past months had produced one experience with YHWH after another. Moses observed this

Being's power and reliability and talked with him on the mountain; but here, at the foot of Horeb, the mountain of YHWH, Moses asked the question that would provide the noontime of revelation in his life. What generated this question that probes for the heart of all existence? Would I ask that question? Would you? "Who are you God? What are you like?" Many people settle for lesser questions. But Moses gained the ear of YHWH and surges for the highest and best with his request. Do you suppose he had any clue how great the answer would be.

The Back Parts of God

God signed the contract! Soon glory would shine and a new revelation would come. Listen to how YHWH put it:

> And he said, I will make all my goodness pass before thee, and I will proclaim the name of the LORD before thee; and will be gracious to whom I will be gracious, and will shew mercy on whom I will shew mercy. And he said, Thou canst not see my face: for there shall no man see me, and live. ...there is a place by me, and thou shalt stand upon a rock: And it shall come to pass, while my glory passeth by, that I will put thee in a clift of the rock, and will cover thee with my hand while I pass by: And I will take away mine hand, and thou shalt see my back parts: but my face shall not be seen. Exodus 33:19-23

This revelation was more than Moses bargained for and more than he could handle. Yes, he would see the glory of YHWH, sort of, to his great danger, but look at the words now associated with that glory—Name, Goodness, Face. YHWH is about to define his glory using these concepts, honoring Moses for the nature of his request. This request to see the glory of YHWH revealed the reality of the friendship of Moses with God.

Had I been Moses and received this offer from God, I would have asked for a house in Hawaii where I could get some relief from these complaining escapees. But, No, what he wanted most was to see the YHWH with whom he had such intimate conversations. The cloud that led these foot-draggers through the wilderness, though associated with his presence, was not the glory of full revelation and Moses knew that. Intense friendship demanded the real thing.

I have often wondered, "Just what is his glory like, anyway?" Its brightness and power brought worship and ministry to a halt in the Tabernacle and the Temple when they were dedicated. That is a captivating thought. This "glory" paralyzed the shepherds when the angels announced the birth of Jesus. This "glory" held the seldom-silent apostle Peter speechless in its presence during a strange event called the Transfiguration. These stunning events wrap "glory" in a mysterious package that leaves one wondering if "glory" is some gale-force Hollywood-type fog that will melt your face if you dare look at it.

But, if glory were merely a cloud, Moses would have been satisfied with the cloud...and he wasn't! Something more was on the way. It didn't take long. YHWH speaks again:

The Unbalanced God

...I will make all my goodness pass before thee... Exodus 33:19

"All that is the very best of me in the widest sense of the word" is going to pass in front of you. (My paraphrase)

Let the parade begin! Roll every parade of history into one! Bring every marching band of all time to the assembly grounds! Gather every float that ever won a prize! Horsemen, ride! Fireworks, bloom!

Our best spectacular, our finest colossal, our most exceedingly stupendous parade of parades shamefully bows and hides in the presence of the Divine parade of "all my goodness!" Sheer logic says that we must lay our miserable egos down in surrender as his flag approaches.

I instinctively know, aware as I am of my guilt, that an appearance of God to me will be negative and confrontive, so, hearing that "goodness" will pass before me is totally disarming. *Blame* walks with me as a deadly traveling companion. I must watch this dangerous *Blame* closely, so closely that he occupies most of my time leaving little time to know God. I reason that, since *Blame* is so threatening, God must be terrifying and must be avoided at all costs. While I walk in the dim light of my feeble understanding, I suspect that God is working behind my back or in my blind spots. To have him walk in front of me—open, revealing—stretches my old concepts past the breaking point.

As I squint in the brightness of this new light, one observation must not escape me—*his goodness is wrapped in his glory*: To know one is to know the other. Good (not bad) hid behind this cloud that protected the Children of Israel and communicated with them. Indeed, there is no indication of a balance in his nature. Often I have argued that one must balance the Law and Grace and sought that balance in my own life only to discover that God seems to lack the very balance I sought. No converses, no opposites, no Yin and Yang are held out to us, no law balanced by grace, no good balanced with evil, no "on the one hand and then on the other hand." His very nature is an unbalanced good.

My Name

...I will proclaim the name of the LORD before thee... Exodus 33:19

A definition approaches! The promise of revelation finds the remaining compartments of our minds and fills them to capacity. YHWH, El Shaddai, God Almighty, I AM WHO I AM, LORD, The Name—subject now of a proclamation, a sermon. I wish I had this sermon on tape!

Something about this name will not let me go. An "open sesame" to the universe reaches out to tell me things beyond my knowing. *Major importance* flashes on the screen of my mind. We will hear something for the first time—a definition of his name. Just as YHWH told Moses in Exodus 6 that he was the first to know his name, now for the first time, the Name will be something more than an identification tag. Also, God stated to Moses that this name was his forever, by choice, reinforcing its uniqueness for us.

Something *more* marches in these letters—YHWH. We do not yet know what the *more* is in the progression of this study. We only know that the play will soon begin and the title on the marquee reads "YHWH."

When I know your name, I own a part of you. If your name is Steve, by calling your name, "Steve," I can bring you to a stop on a busy street or across a crowded, noisy room and have your complete attention. But the ownership is merely temporary and interruptive, an ownership of attention. What can happen next once you have shouted a name? Can a conversation begin? Not unless you know the person. Unless you know the person, the arrest of attention merely exercises your vocal cords. The next question is, "What value is there in knowing the meaning of a person's name?"

In the days of Moses, a name was significant precisely because of its meaning. Names, somehow, were assigned in accordance with the nature or promise of the person. Thus, to know a person's name and the meaning of the name was to truly know the person. Whereas we, with modern traditions, merely search through books of names. We find one or two names that sound good and will look good in theater lights giving little, if any, heed to the meaning of the name. But God gives meaning to his name and to all whom he names.

Glory Is My Name Is My Glory

A new contract of ownership unrolls for Moses (and us) as YHWH prepares to preach the meaning of his name. It seems too much for us that the mysteries of the meaning of the eternal name of God soon will be ours.

Another thought approaches and must not be permitted to escape. YHWH chooses to attach the meaning of his name to the revelation of his glory. His Name and his Glory walk together. To know one is to know the other. To know him is to know his Glory is to know his Name is to know his Goodness. They cannot, must not, be separated.

Indeed, the highest of our insights arrives—his Name and his Goodness must be the description, the definition of his Glory—the very thing that Moses wanted most to see. If so, we have stumbled onto knowledge that shakes and shapes all we do. To define his Glory is to define his Name is to define his Nature. Glory now touches my beliefs, my prayer, my actions, even these fingers as they write this manuscript. Too much! Surely this is fatal knowledge.

Mercy, Mercy

...and will be gracious to whom I will be gracious, and will shew mercy on whom I will shew mercy. Exodus 33:19

Lest we misunderstand, YHWH enlarges his first statement to Moses about his goodness. Now he assures Moses of mercy and compassion. Lest Moses misinterpret, it must be repeated that God is not balanced (as we understand balance). He is goodness in its best and widest sense; he is mercy and compassion; he is YHWH. Lest we forget.

The breaking point has come. Death surely must hover near. One cannot hear and know these things and stay alive.

Danger

...Thou canst not see my face: ...and live. Exodus 33:20

The frightening truth rolls out. It is, indeed, too much for us, pushing us to our mortal limits. In spite of the goodness of his glory and his name, we come quickly to a halt! Dare we pull the curtain and look around? Dare we hope that something better waits behind. The cloud was our umbrella saving us from his face. There is an extremity to goodness, mercy and compassion beyond the limits of mortal experience. "Our God is a consuming fire." (Deuteronomy 4:24) Our hearts burn and melt in pools of shame before his pure goodness. Who will rescue us? Can knowing him only produce death?

Foundation Rock

...there is a place by me, and thou shalt stand upon a rock: ...while my glory passeth by, that I will put thee in a clift of the rock, and will cover thee with my hand while I pass by:.... Exodus 33:21,22

We should have known! The God, who commanded the sacrifice of Isaac then provided the lamb himself at the last minute, has not changed. Now, in the face of death, he provides for us a rock on which to stand and in which to hide. The rock is near him. His own hand will provide the covering. I cannot find the rock by seeking it out, nor would safety be my guarantee were I to crouch in some crevice of my own discovering. YHWH provides the rock that is comfortably near him; YHWH knows the brokenness in the rock which is ideal for those who must be hidden; YHWH provides the protection. "Oh, God of all creation, where can I flee but to you."

Images flood my mind:
"The rock which the builders rejected has become the cornerstone."

"...upon this rock I will build my church and the gates of hell shall not prevail against it."
"...the Shepherd, the Rock of Israel."
"Strike the rock, and water will come."
"He is the Rock, his works are perfect."
"The Lord is my rock, my fortress..."
"Lead me to the rock that is higher than I."

He *will* pass by, and the only limitation placed on this contract of revelation is designed to protect our lives. Typical YHWH. But, in the protection YHWH offers, a problem arises. How can Moses see him and yet not see him? Ah, it takes one with higher thoughts to decipher this dilemma. Let us see how YHWH resolves this one.

> And I will take away mine hand, and thou shalt see my back parts: but my face shall not be seen. Exodus 33:23

The back parts of God! So that is how he would protect us and keep us alive. This "Almighty," this "God of fire," this "YHWH," this "God of glory," this "God who reveals himself" is also the "God of the protecting hand." But his back parts? This sounds a little embarrassing. Is God, perhaps, making a statement about my humanity? Yes, but to see him is to see him and that is enough.

Now, Moses has work to do. Meeting royalty always requires strenuous preparations, but this is the King of all creation. However, the instructions are simple and Moses sets about his task.

Take Two Tablets

My imagination readily reconstructs the scene. Chiseling stone plates relieved Moses' mind from the intensity of his earlier conversation with YHWH, but he must have had trouble concentrating. Beneath his exhaustion mysteries played across his thoughts. "Are these stones merely a repeat of the first ones?" The earlier trip—"Ah, it seemed so long ago"—produced plates like these, but...memory awakened the rage that caused him to destroy the first plates and a blush at the wave of shame he felt. "I saw him make the first tablets. How will this time be different?"

Hammer blows, inspection, more chipping, then satisfaction. Moses placed the plates carefully in the corner of his tent. Carrying them up the mountain would not be easy since he had to go alone and, after all, he was eighty years old, so he hoped that sleep would come quickly to his worn body. Though he could see as well as ever and his physical relationship with his wife had not lessened (Deuteronomy 34:7); he was in his eighties and it took its toll. He heard the claps of someone at his tent door and rose to greet the welcome face of Joshua.

THE FATHER STYLE

Part Two

THE MOUNTAIN

Mountain Majesty

"Joshua, tomorrow is going to be a day unlike any I have ever experienced. I have some specific instructions to give you. First, we must remove all cattle from around Horeb. God has warned me not to have even a cow there. Nor can any people remain there. Treat the mountain as if it were deadly."

"I will pass the word quickly so no one will leave early to graze there. I think I am going to enjoy this journey with you."

"Sorry, Joshua, but that is the other instruction. I must go alone. This time you are not permitted to come. That is what YHWH said to me today."

"I am sorry, too, but I will get the information to the people tonight."

"Remember, Joshua, no one is to be seen on the mountain. Good night."

The tent flaps closed behind Joshua as he left and Moses sank to his mat for welcome sleep. Finally, his exhaustion overcame his racing thoughts and time awaited his predawn awakening for tomorrow's monumental task.

The regular thump of his walking stick greeted the approaching light of day as Moses picked his way along the familiar path up Mt. Horeb, tablets in hand, anticipation on his face.

He wished that others could walk with him, but YHWH was not seen as a friend by most of the people in the camp and their terror washed away any desire to hear from him (See "Leave Us Alone" in Part Five). "And he says I must come alone. No time to worry about that now, though." The familiar climb took so little of his attention that his mind was free to ponder the coming event. Excitement levels rose with each step. In his years in Egypt and the desert, he had seen almost everything there was to see and few things excited him any more, but this moment exceeded everything the earth, as he knew it, could offer.

One last incline of steps opened into the worn boulders and walls that marked the summit. His memory flashed with the drama of former meetings with YHWH while his eagerness for this meeting grew as he picked his way toward the place he instinctively knew would be the spot. Breathing swiftly from the climb and his emotion, he reached his destination and leaned back to rest and wait in a split rock, a cave, that seemed to be designed just for resting.

Suddenly, the cloud! That intimate cloud that led them, that flamed, that faced him and spoke in the tent, that listened, that separated them from their enemies, that was thick darkness and light at the same time, began to form at the opening of this rock taking a new shape that bent around the rock and covered it completely. Light filled every corner of his crevice so that there were no shadows and Moses could see the ridges and furrows that let him know a hand had covered his spot. Then it happened. God passed by and defined or preached or explained or proclaimed his name and his glory:

> Then the LORD came down in the cloud and stood there with him and proclaimed his name, the LORD. And he passed in front of Moses, proclaiming, "The LORD, the LORD, the compassionate and gracious God, slow to anger, abounding in love and faithfulness, maintaining love to thousands, and forgiving wickedness, rebellion and sin. Yet he does not leave the guilty unpunished; he punishes the children and their children for the sin of the fathers to the third and fourth generation."
> Exodus 34:5-7 NIV

Here, God, by defining his name, was revealing the very essence of his being. That makes this passage too profound to lightly pass. God is revealing his traits as the meaning of his name and his glory. Let us draw closer and look at the components that define his name.

Compassionate

This is action, not just state of being. Pity, by itself, is an unfulfilled promise demanding no action on our part. God, who moves beyond mere pity, is not speaking from his safe Heaven saying, "I feel so sorry for you. It must be tough." No, this compassion is pity that moves him to do something about our situation. This compassion is the "tender mercy" that a father would show toward his child—almost a mercy that permits itself to be manipulated, taken advantage of. Compassion is more than a feeling; it moves God. Jesus was "moved with compassion" for the multitudes because he saw them as sheep without a shepherd. As a result, Jesus was willing to teach the crowd for days while knowing that they would misunderstand.

This "tender mercy" keeps God's face turned toward us even though we keep getting his message wrong and living inadequately. This compassion fuels the grace that causes God to let the sun shine on the righteous and the unrighteous.

This very first trait that God reveals about himself places him beyond the limitations imposed by those (such as Deists) who feel that God merely "wound up" the universe and now has little interaction or concern for it. He may have "wound up" the universe, but now he carefully intervenes in our behalf.

Gracious

This word is simply what it says, gracious. When God is gracious, he is giving us what we do not deserve. He pours out his goodness to us. We all benefit from this trait of God and benefit so profoundly and frequently that we have become surfeited and spoiled to his kindness. We take him for granted. Were we to express gratitude for every moment of grace, our entire time would be devoted to "Thank you."

A friend of mine, responding to God's statement that his thoughts for us are "as the sands of the sea," (Psalms 139:17,18) attempted to calculate how many thoughts that would represent for each person. His result, which I consider to be on the conservative side, was approximately seven thoughts for each of us each second. Since we know that God's thoughts for us are good (Jeremiah 29:11), that means that God thinks seven good thoughts for us each second of our lives. With this many good thoughts from God, I have no need to even think of myself.

On numerous occasions, I have miraculously been delayed on freeways to later discover that I had been spared a major accident, or routed away from planes that would be involved in accidents. Sometimes I am frustrated at the change of plans, then elated at how God has protected me. When I see such protection occur, I realize that this is a *visible* evidence of his grace. Then I realize this is merely visible evidence. I wonder how many times God has saved my life and I didn't even know it? Probably uncountable.

Perhaps, when I get to Heaven, God will say, "Gayle's here, huh? Put in the video of his life and let him see just how much trouble I had protecting him all these years!" We are people spoiled by his grace. I like it. I plan to be more grateful.

God seems to labor so hard to make sure we see that his giving nature goes beyond compassion, thus he reveals himself to be onesided and unbalanced at the same time. Confession time again! Remember the argument, "We must strive for balance in our lives." This is an argument to which I give agreement even while feeling some pangs of misgiving. Remember, also, my earlier statement of belief, "God by his very nature is unbalanced." We must probe this idea further.

Mercy and grace by definition are onesided and unbalanced. If we think we must balance our righteousness with God's mercy, we deceive ourselves. We have no righteousness, we have only his mercy. If we think we must balance our mercy toward others with some other trait, we mock our own prayer, "forgive our trespasses as we forgive those who trespass against us." John 3:16 does *not* say "For God so loved the world that he 'struck a deal' with it."

God's mercies are so lavish that he chooses to make them new every day (Lamentations 3:23), a fact that irrevocably removes all chance of balance in this universe. God is not a slave to entropy, the law of physics that says that all things are running down and coming to an equilibrium. He still moves creatively adding the energy of his mercy to our lives, removing the warp and kindling a peaceful tension.

Slow to Anger

Only the true and living God is longsuffering. Untrue gods created by men are assumed to be angry and we must only figure out how to appease them. The true God knows us to be guilty and works hard at making his forgiveness available to us.

Do you ever think that God is gritting his teeth as he looks at you and is saying, "Just one more time, buddy, just one more time, then bam!"? That is not the way he views us. Instead, his grace is renewed every morning! That seems too good to be true. God, against whom we sin relentlessly (and we are powerless to change that), knows that he made us out of dirt and is careful to keep his store of favor from running out by restocking it every morning. It is good that he does not slumber or sleep!

Jesus successfully resisted Satan's attempt to get him to "test" or "tempt" God. I do not so successfully resist. There are so many ways I press the edges of his mercy that I cannot list them all, but a few come quickly to mind.

I test God with the routines I use to find his will. Gideon, the Old Testament coward-turned-warrior, exhibited his faithlessness by making God prove his will with a fleece that was to be alternately wet then dry on successive nights. We, having found this fascinating incident, blindly join him in his failure by demanding that God fulfill some "test" we give him in order to satisfy ourselves. By applying the "Nature of Jesus" test to this episode (see Part Four), one can immediately discern that such "fleecing" is purely for our own comfort (thus selfish) and not for the sake of the ministry or the call.

God must know me as "the great demander!" Like clockwork, when he speaks to me and asks me to do something for him, I am quick to inform him of my willingness to do so and will obey as soon as he makes adequate advance provision for me. Again, I am testing him.

Any "normal" human being would have abandoned or obliterated me, but the God of Compassion and Grace patiently waits for my inch-by-inch progress. Even in the presence of those who seem to get it right when I don't, he never scolds me. He simply gives liberally to the lacking ones who come with their requests held out in front of them. Ah, the God with the smiling, not the angry, face.

Perhaps, since anger so accurately reflects the human situation, we (who tend to shape our gods into our image) find it beyond our comprehension that the true God, the one who shaped us in *his* image, would be longsuffering.

> The Lord is not slack concerning his promise, as some count slackness; but is longsuffering to us-ward, not willing that any should perish, but that all should come to repentance. 2 Peter 3:9

We can now gloat in our rest, wallow in our joyous circumstance.

Abounding in Mercy and Faithfulness

I choose to translate "checed" as mercy in this statement, because that is its most frequently found form. "Checed" is translated "love" in the next section, although mercy is the stronger.

Not merely adequate, but abounding is this great God of glory. His barns and silos overflow with mercy and faithfulness; he stacks it in the streets looking for a distribution system. He "lavishes" on us. (Ephesians 1:7,8 NIV)

Mercy is the centerpiece of all heaven. Mercy is what heaven is all about. Mercy is when God does not give us what we deserve. If he did, we would all be burnt crisps by now. Instead, he lavishes mercy on us.

Mercy is not a source of pain for God. God is not irritated at the fact that he must issue mercy. It is more natural for God to issue mercy than it is for a child to play or a dog to bark.

Declarations about God abound; many cases are made for him daily. Something about the word "preacher" denotes in the popular mind a grim, judgmental face growling out the word "barrimstoneuh" with barely concealed glee. Partly as a result of this kind of stereotype and partly because of our own simple knowledge of our guilt, we have come to view God as our enemy, the spoiler of the cosmic party, the "boss" in the sky.

Nothing could be farther from the truth!

This very declaration to Moses that we are examining gives a powerful clue to his central nature. The Tabernacle he instructed Moses to construct draws all the clues together and permits only one conclusion—the centerpiece of all Heaven is mercy! The Tabernacle of the wilderness was only a copy of the true one in Heaven (Hebrews 9:24) thus its effects were temporary and symbolic.

The main feature, the feature most revered and most sought, the feature around which the whole scheme was fixed is the Holy of Holies. Its furnishing was solely the Ark of the Covenant whose central focus was a place between the hovering wings of cherubim—a place known as the "Mercy Seat." That annually-and-cautiously accessible place called the "Mercy Seat" was but a symbol of its replacement—the constantly-and-boldly accessible presence and nature of our God through Jesus Christ.

How have we managed to escape this central truth through the ages? How have we managed to be set free from the law only to build another law by our mishandling of the realities of God? Our attempts to keep the old law or even to build a new religious law is arrogant humanism. I am sure that any religious legalist of this day would resent my calling him a humanist, since you might find him on the forefront of the fight against secular humanism, but religious humanism is a far more serious matter—causing mankind to think that his efforts in any way would merit God's favor. Jesus hurled some strong statements against that kind of humanism. (Mark 7:9, Matthew 23:23)

It was this mercy that David declared to be better than life (Psalm 63:3, translated as love or loving kindness). Perhaps such knowledge of the central character of God and centerpiece of the universe made David the man he was. Indeed, David spoke often of God's mercy—the Psalms are laced with mercy. That very fact brings up an interesting human dichotomy:

David was known as a warrior, yet his Psalms are so full of peace and grace. The people sang of his killing tens of thousands (typical hero worship). It might even be concluded by some of those hero worshipers that God chose the throne of David to endure forever because he was so strong and such a warrior. Yet David's Psalms are not filled with such songs of self-serving bravado. Interesting that the folk songs of heroics were not canonized and do not live today. Instead, we hear of the God of mercy. David sings it over and over as if entranced. Psalm 103 is the song of a dancing soul for whom God has pulled aside the curtain of time to let him see the fullness of eternal purpose and divine nature. Let it speak for itself:

> Bless the LORD, O my soul: and all that is within me, bless his holy name. Bless the LORD, O my soul, and forget not all his benefits: Who forgiveth all thine iniquities; who healeth all thy diseases; Who redeemeth thy life from destruction; who crowneth

thee with lovingkindness and tender mercies; Who satisfieth thy mouth with good things; so that thy youth is renewed like the eagle's.

The LORD executeth righteousness and judgment for all that are oppressed. He made known his ways unto Moses, his acts unto the children of Israel. The LORD is merciful and gracious, slow to anger, and plenteous in mercy. He will not always chide: neither will he keep his anger for ever. He hath not dealt with us after our sins; nor rewarded us according to our iniquities.

For as the heaven is high above the earth, so great is his mercy toward them that fear him. As far as the east is from the west, so far hath he removed our transgressions from us. Like as a father pitieth his children, so the LORD pitieth them that fear him. For he knoweth our frame; he remembereth that we are dust.

As for man, his days are as grass: as a flower of the field, so he flourisheth. For the wind passeth over it, and it is gone; and the place thereof shall know it no more. But the mercy of the LORD is from everlasting to everlasting upon them that fear him, and his righteousness unto children's children; To such as keep his covenant, and to those that remember his commandments to do them.

Dance, my soul, dance!

For years, I thought that repentance came when sufficient pressure was applied to someone. If I could adequately shake someone over the fire, I could extract promises and changes from him. To surround with threat was to have successfully preached. How wrong I was! A body blow from the pen of the Apostle Paul left me reeling, and I still have not recovered. He said, "...God's kindness leads you toward repentance." (Romans 2:4) So! It is not my adeptness at producing guilt that produces repentance! No, it is only his mercy. When I do not likewise show mercy then I fulfill the first part of the verse above, showing "...contempt for the riches of his kindness, tolerance and patience..." (Romans 2:4) That whole concept frightens us. We think that if we don't keep heavy pressure on the wayward human spirit, God will lose control of the world and the Church. If God invented mercy, surely he knows how to use it in our lives.

If we must come down on one side of the fence, God help us to come down on the side of mercy. We who struggle in our walk, often feel that God directs a band of angels especially trained in karate, two of whom are assigned to each of us. Now we gloat in our rest, wallow in our joyous circumstance, plunge headlong into this ocean that never evaporates. Come on in; the water's fine!

We hope for people to be merciful enough and to be faithful enough, but God abounds in these qualities. My bank may call itself "fidelity" or "faithful" but I still read the annual report with serious skepticism. I may hear that the product has a one-year or lifetime guarantee, but, instinctively, I know there is a catch somewhere.

We learn to distrust, because life and humanity have carefully taught us to distrust.

I blush at the thought of how many promises I have made and how few I have fulfilled. When you ask someone if I can be trusted, he may pause before he answers, but not so with God; you can count on him. Scripture echoes with statements about God's faithfulness. Moses calls him "a faithful God who does no wrong." (Deuteronomy 32:4 NIV) Psalms declares "The works of his hands are faithful," (111:7 NIV) "The LORD is faithful to all his promises," (145:13 NIV) and "The LORD...remains faithful forever." (146:6 NIV)

Paul tells us, "God is faithful; he will not let you be tempted beyond what you can bear." (1 Corinthians 10:13 NIV) "The one who calls you is faithful and he will do it." (1 Thessalonians 5:24 NIV) "But Christ is faithful as a son over God's house." (Hebrews 3:6 NIV) "Let us hold unswervingly to the hope we profess, for he who promised is faithful." (Hebrews 10:23 NIV) "By faith Abraham,...was enabled to become a father because he considered him faithful who had made the promise." (Hebrews 11:11 NIV)

John lofts our hearts with this declaration: "If we confess our sins, he is faithful and just and will forgive us our sins and purify us from all unrighteousness." (1 John 1:9 NIV) In John's great Revelation of Jesus Christ, he called Jesus the "faithful witness" (1:5), "the Amen, the faithful and true witness," (3:14) the rider of the white horse who is called, "Faithful and True." (19:11)

My life is one of traveling, and, though it has its difficulties, certain benefits are overwhelming. I have the privilege of meeting many people and hearing their testimonies of God's faithfulness. Some groups will spend hours in collective awe as one after another will report on hopeless situations that were restored in a faithful act of God. Sometimes spontaneous applause erupts as God *comes through* in one of these reports. One would think we were trying to encourage God...and maybe we are! There would not even be a word "faithful" if it were not for God.

Usually we human beings have to be driven to faithfulness either by threat or by law. Abounding faithfulness falls outside our scope of hope or achievement. Booming abandonment, jammed divorce courts and the phenomenon called "living together" proves our love as fickle as the wind. Vows designed for a lifetime are shattered within hours. Love is written in our instincts, yet erased by our actions. God knew we were as powerless to teach ourselves as two inebriates would be to lift each other up, so he sent his Son who is just like him to model faithfulness for us.

Maintaining Love to Thousands

Love, a subject too large for this modest book, would also not exist were it not for the God who is Love. (1 John 4:8) My wife likes to hear the words "I love you" from me every day. Something about my inadequacy causes her to need that frequent assurance.

The difficulty is that we humans believe ourselves to be good at love. After once reading what seemed to be a logical book about situation ethics, I was plagued by the thesis: "No rule fits every situation, so let me view the situation, decide the loving thing and do it." The author deftly showed instances in which each of the Ten Commandments would not be correct to follow. The book nagged me for days. I was sure one could not so easily dismiss the Ten Commandments. There must be a flaw somewhere. Then I found it! The flaw is me, Gayle Erwin. You cannot turn me loose on a situation to decide what the loving thing is. My mind is so scrambled by self interest that I cannot be trusted to know the loving thing to do in all circumstances. Scripture even says, "The heart is deceitful above all things, and desperately wicked: who can know it?" (Jeremiah 17:9) Long before the "country/western" song writer, the Bible called it "Your Cheating Heart!"

So I am the flaw. I cannot know within myself what the loving act would be. Someone who does know must teach me. Again, the one who abounds in mercy and faithfulness steps into our degraded lives to let his Son show us how to love. Then, this Jesus simply tells us to love the same way he has loved. Now, as we look at him, we have the pattern of love—servanthood. *For the full treatment of this theme, read **The Jesus Style** by Gayle D. Erwin published by Word Books, Dallas, Texas.*

The simple face value of these words "love to thousands" can be staggering. Everything we own must be maintained. Entropy reduced even Rome's grandeur to a pile of curious ruins. Relationships, when ignored, collapse. With every item one purchases goes the concern about service; enough so that service contracts have become a major commercial item. It takes but few possessions to absorb all of our time and energy in maintenance.

God, on the other hand, maintains his love toward us with limitless time and energy; and, lest we feel that our position is perilous, he maintains that love to thousands! One can almost sense God struggling with the limits of our language to inform us that no number of people and no distance in time from this revelation will begin to tax the resources of his love toward us.

Intricate and persistent repairs occur in any breaches that Satan may make in that love. When one suffers or is disappointed or bruised, the healing process begins immediately. The "balm of Gilead" is strongly attracted to open wounds. Even the badly wounded person would, if sensitive to the definition of his God, find that the evidence of his maintaining love showed early in the battle.

Abundance of mercy, as we saw in previous discussions, means that God cannot be limited to the immediate or to "me." His love overflows to thousands. How well this is borne out in Isaiah 53 with these statements: "my righteous servant will justify many" (11); "he bore the sins of many." (12) The good news has never been a private reserve. Something in its very nature begs to be released to the thousands. Even persecution, to the dismay of the enemies of God, cannot begin to suppress the Gospel. Indeed, the greater the pressure of persecution, the greater the distance the resultant explosion sends the good news. God's love is for "many." Somehow, it will be delivered to them.

I have a rabbi friend who tells me that the better translation for this scripture is "maintaining love to the thousands generations," and some translations state it that way. I like that. If a generation is forty years (and that is just an educated guess on our part) then a thousand generations would be 40,000 years and "thousands" generations would be at least 120,000 years. How is God going to do that? I don't know how God is going to do that, but I like it! All our feelings of worthlessness must pale in the knowledge that, at least, our relationship with God has started a long trail of blessing.

Forgiving

...and forgiving wickedness, rebellion and sin. Exodus 34:7

Were we to stop with what we have already discovered about "all his goodness," we would be more than blessed. What more could we ask than to have a God who is compassionate, gracious, slow to anger, abounding in mercy and faithfulness and maintaining love to thousands? But we have merely stuck a toe into the ocean of his abundance. This great YHWH also forgives wickedness, rebellion and sin.

In case you think "wicked" doesn't really describe you, God has you covered—he forgives rebellion, also. If you feel "rebellion" doesn't really describe you, God still has you covered, he forgives sin, also. Aha! Now he has us!

This statement is a Hebrew idiom that means "All sins. All types and manner of sins." It leaves out nothing. Let me list some synonyms for these words so you can see the depth of his forgiveness:

> Corruption, depravity, dishonesty, immorality, impurity, vice, wrong, anarchy, terrorism, crime, dishonor, disobedience, evil, fault, felony, infamy, infraction, iniquity, injury, lawbreaking, misdeed, misdemeanor, offense, outrage, transgression, trespass, violation, fall

Each one of us grovels somewhere in the list above. Perhaps most of us feel that our sins are beyond God's forgiveness. How often I have heard men describe their own sins that way. Actually, arrogance causes us to believe that we have sins in the "special category" of "too big to be forgiven by God." However, God even forgives arrogance. Luke 6:35 reveals, "...for he is kind unto the unthankful and to the evil." Amazing.

This forgiveness is love and mercy in action, also. So strong is this trait that from a cruel, man-made, agonizing cross of death, Jesus could say, "Father, forgive them. They don't know what they are doing." The overwhelming understanding, though, is that God forgives us even when we *do know* what we are doing. All we have to do is turn our hearts toward him—confess, repent—and God does the rest. There is nothing too hard for him.

Punishment

> Yet he does not leave the guilty unpunished; he punishes the children and their children for the sin of the fathers to the third and fourth generation. Exodus 34:7

This passage seems, on the surface, incompatible with the prior expression of the meaning and nature of the Name of God. It is not quoted in the places where it would most likely be quoted by later writers. It seems out of keeping with the nature of Jesus. One major problem has to do with the nature of mankind.

As I share with men these passages from Exodus about the nature of God, a general excitement and hopefulness turns a light on in their hearts, mounts a sparkle in the eye. Then I read this passage that speaks of punishment being visited upon the children. The eyes darken as I see men's minds go over the sins of their past. In fear they wonder what their children are going to have to suffer because of what they have done—even though they have been redeemed!

Suddenly, grace takes a back seat. I feel dirty and ashamed as if I have done God a disservice and inaccurately portrayed him. There are several ways to handle this apparent paradox and I share them in the order of my own preference.

A Major Problem and an Audacious Proposal

First, this judgment passage may have been translated opposite to its meaning. Translators and commentators are not unanimous in their positions that the words recorded are the actual translation. Some feel that this is an idiom used that expresses the exact opposite of what is recorded. This would make the statement read, "He forgives the guilty and visits his forgiveness on children and their children for the sake of the father to the third and fourth generations." Does it sound too good to be true? If so, perhaps we are getting closer to the reality of God, especially when we see him in the face of Jesus.

Second, this passage may have been merely mistranslated or misunderstood.

Matthew Henry states the following:

> Some read it so as to express a mitigation of wrath, even when he does punish: **When he empties, he will not make quite desolate;** that is, "He does not proceed to the greatest extremity, till there be no remedy." Vol. 1, p 425

Some translators quote it as follows: "who in destroying will not wholly destroy." Others (Geddes, for instance) take it even further: "who acquits even him who is not innocent."

Whatever tack is taken about this passage, commentators seem driven to have to explain. Why would the God of the first part (compassion, forgiveness) also be the God of the second part (punishment)? Little explanation is needed for the first expression of his grace. Those statements of grace are self-evident sources of great rejoicing. But the second part, for some reason, needs clarification, since, at least to some readers, it sets the heart on a different course than the first part.

Some argue that, without the second part, the first part is meaningless, that is, without judgment, mercy is without meaning. I would agree except that God's judgment is not destroyed by the changing of this statement. He is still God and can develop judgment in any way he wishes, even when he leaves us to the natural consequences of our own action. But visiting sins of the fathers on innocent progeny? That does not match the justice that even God declares for himself. Indeed, we see that the presence of only a handful of righteous people would have spared the city of Sodom.

Jonah would certainly have been aware of this passage. In his disdain for the inhabitants of Nineveh, why didn't he quote this passage to God and call upon him to fulfill it? Is it because, in actuality, Jonah knew it merely reinforced the mercy that had been stated before and needed no further quoting?

Also, God's love allows sinful man the ability to choose. At a point, God "gives us over" to the sinful desires of our hearts. (Romans 1:24) The natural consequence would be an unending series of punishment to myself and my progeny. But God's mercy limits the punishment to three or four generations.

An example might be the household of Saul. Saul's sin of rebellion and disobedience (1 Samuel 15:22-23) resulted in:

1. Saul's suicide (1 Samuel 31:4)

2. Death of his sons including Jonathan (1 Samuel 31:6)

3. Jonathan's son Mephibosheth crippled (2 Samuel 9:3), but he ate in the house of David (2 Samuel 9:11).

4. Mephibosheth had a son Mica who ate at David's table and no infirmity is recorded for him. (2 Samuel 9:12)

A third possibility, and the most commonly held, is that this is simply the fate reserved only for those who remain defiantly unredeemed. Strong evidence for this explanation exists in Deuteronomy 5:9 and 7:9,10 and Ezekiel 18:20. In Deuteronomy, as God restates the punishment passage, such punishment is reserved only for those who hate God. So, if you don't hate God, the mercy passage applies to you and not the punishment passage. This is especially encouraging for Christians who suffer the guilt from the teaching that targets for punishment because of the misdeeds of an ancestor.

Unquestionably, the overriding trait we see of God is his compassion. Even kings who did every conceivable wicked thing they could, who by all rights should have been destroyed, found themselves forgiven of God when they called upon his name. Then certainly mercy is "all his goodness."

So how can we free the redeemed from the terror of this passage? Perhaps this is the "terror of the Lord" that caused the Apostle Paul to "persuade men" (1 Corinthians 5) once he saw the full nature of God in Jesus. I choose to believe that the Deuteronomy passages that restrict punishment to those who hate God provide adequate understanding of the meaning and freedom from fear. I can rest in his mercy and the justice wrought on my sins by the Cross of Christ.

If we choose to explain the punishment passage as a necessary element to balance the expression of grace and if we apply it only to the unredeemed, we have created another difficult problem. This passage does not actually say or imply such a balance. No disclaimer exists protecting the forgiven, only punishment for sin. This leaves us with God punishing the redeemed which is unthinkable and impossible because of the sacrifice of Jesus.

My rabbi friend claims the odds are still in our favor—love is for "thousands" generations and punishment is only for four generations.

Again, I find myself coming to the conclusion that the very nature of grace is unbalanced. I must cease trying to bring God to my scales to balance him.

A fourth possibility is that this passage represents the death that mankind bought for himself in the garden which haunts us and binds us until we are released by the death and resurrection of Jesus himself. Evidence arrives in Colossians 1:19-22:

> For God was pleased to have all his fullness dwell in him, and through him to reconcile to himself all things, whether things on earth or things in heaven, by making peace through his blood, shed on the cross.
> Once you were alienated from God and were enemies in your minds because of your evil behavior. But now he has reconciled you by Christ's physical body through death to present you holy in his sight, without blemish and free from accusation. NIV

The writer of Hebrews seems to be trying to affirm our release from the curse of death and punishment with his explanation of the sacrifice of Jesus in comparison to the sacrifice of animals. Simply put, one (The sacrifice is Jesus) is effective in establishing our relationship with God and the other (animal sacrifices) isn't.

> But in those sacrifices there is a remembrance again made of sins every year. For it is not possible that the blood of bulls and

> of goats should take away sins.
> Hebrews 10:3,4
>
> By the which will we are sanctified through the offering of the body of Jesus Christ once for all. 10

Whatever our belief about the judgment passage, we find that somehow we need relief from the face of an avenging God. At the very least, God has and is holding man accountable for his actions and his response to God. However, if for some reason, we find that he is not avenging at all, then, perhaps, we can "come boldly before his throne of grace." As the last seconds tick off in the Old Testament, God sweeps us again into a state of high hope as he says:

> But for you who revere my name, the sun of righteousness will rise with healing in its wings. And you will go out and leap like calves released from the stall.
> Malachi 4:2 NIV

The Name, the Name

Now we have the definitions of both the Name and the Glory of YHWH. His grace rolls toward us in waves that drown our sin. We can build a Tower of Babel as mere human beings, but we cannot build a throne of righteousness. God's edict disrupted our tower and another edict established our righteousness through him. It is too good. Surely God cannot be that good. Surely we are merely fooling ourselves and toying with our own emotions. Surely this is the hopeful dreaming of the mentally incapable.

But, no! Beyond our best dreams, YHWH shows himself good. And this is *only his back parts*. I can understand why his face would have killed Moses.

The tide of understanding rises about the use of the word "Name" in the Bible. Now I can understand why the Name of YHWH would be a strong tower or would be dependable rather than chariots and horses. (Be sure to read the meditations on NAME, FACE and GLORY at the end of this book.) Now dawns the understanding of what it means to have His Name or His Glory on us. The story could end here and Eden would be restored, but, alas, there is more. Never underestimate the power of human beings to destroy Eden.

THE FATHER STYLE

Part Three

THE VALLEY

The Law, the Law

Eternity now strolls the mountain-top of the cleft rock and the hidden Moses. All Goodness reveals himself in his Name and his Glory. The fleeting glimpse of the back of YHWH pushes the mortality of Moses to its limit.

We glance back to that scene in Exodus 34 at the closing moment of the revelation, and Moses is now on his face on the ground worshiping, overwhelmed by this glimpse of the Glory of God. What else can one do in such a circumstance? However, in the midst of this awesome moment, there is something remarkably mercenary in Moses. Since YHWH is *this* good, perhaps Moses can push against some of *His* limits. In possession of such hidden knowledge, Moses knows that Israel is without a future unless the YHWH accompanies, so he attempts another deal.

> "Go with us. I know we are stubborn, but go with us. Forgive us when we sin accidentally and purposefully. And hang on to us as your inheritance." Exodus 34:9

Anxious moments pass as Moses waits for the answer. Had he pushed too far? Perhaps he should have been satisfied with simply seeing YHWH. Then God answers.

"You have a contract, Moses. In fact, I'm going to do more great things for you and your people than have been done for all other nations in history. When people look at you they will know I am YHWH." Moses won. The contract was signed.

However, we are about to see another grand scheme, another revelation, another contract that rivals the last. This revelation will also set the course of history and shape the destiny of mankind. In fact, this new revelation will capture our attention and lock it in a narrow tunnel. What can it be? *The Law!*

Earlier, God has revealed his own nature to Moses and mankind, now he begins the commands that sum up the Law. The Law reveals the nature of mankind while The Name reveals the nature of God. Countless laws are needed to handle the nature of humanity. No set of laws can be written against the nature of God. (See Galatians 5.)

In order for human beings to understand how much they needed the mercy (Glory, Nature) of God, he gave them the Law so they would learn that they could not keep the Law and must turn to God for help. (See Hebrews 10:3,4; Romans 8:3; Galatians 3:24.) That sounds like a fair bargain. First, try to keep the Law so you can stay humbly aware of your own inadequacy. Second, come to the Lord with your failure and his mercy will cover it. Excellent deal. But, no deal! Israel would have none of it. Rather than swim in the endless ocean of God's mercy, Israel chose to focus their attention on the Law and their own ability to keep the Law and earn God's favor.

Now, the old "can do" spirit of fallen humanity enters the picture. Somehow we are determined to prove that we can change our ways or turn over a new leaf or earn our keep or master our fate. Now, the watchword was "Law" not "Mercy." Moses would be known as the Lawgiver, not as the Mercy-receiver. The Torah would be a voluminous jot and tittle enlargement of the Law. There would be no similar probe of his mercy.

The sad self-centeredness that began in the Garden of Eden continues to sow weeds.

One-way Covenants

Some of God's covenants such as the one beginning in Exodus 34:10 are "if, then" covenants: "If you will obey, I will bless." However, from the beginning, God knew that man did not have it in him to obey. That is why the major covenants such as Genesis 12 with Abraham are one-way covenants. (This is such an incredible show of God's nature that we must discuss it in a section a few pages later.) God covenants or agrees to bless or to do and places no requirement on mankind.

Amazing! His grace explodes in our eyes but we are too busy watching road hazards to see it. If I see his mercy, that means that I must totally accept my inadequacy and my pride won't let me do that, yet.

Even the "if, then" covenants could only prove to a wise person that God is gracious. Any discerning eye could see that obedience does not reside naturally in mankind, therefore any requirement on us that would result in blessing simply could not be met. Therefore, any blessing that we receive can never be the result of our goodness or *earning* it. Any blessing can only be laid at the door of his grace and mercy, not our adequacy.

Sheer experience and simple wisdom ought to paint that picture of mercy with clarity, but pride is the great eye-cataract of nature. We know something is out there, but we just can't see it through our own flaws.

Ah, but in the middle of the sticky mud of the Law, brilliant flashbacks occur. Signs break forth to prove that deep in the heart of Israel beats eternal evidence of God's nature.

David knew the nature of his God as he reveals in Psalms 103:8, "The LORD is compassionate and gracious, slow to anger, abounding in love."

The writer of Judges in 2:18 knew. He declares: "...for the LORD had compassion on them as they groaned under those who oppressed and afflicted them." NIV

The writer of 2 Kings in 13:23 knew the nature of God. He declares: "And the LORD was gracious unto them, and had compassion on them and had respect unto them, because of his covenant with Abraham, Isaac, and Jacob, and would not destroy them, neither cast he them from his presence as yet."

Isaiah knew. In 30:18, he declares: "Yet the LORD longs to be gracious to you; he rises to show you compassion. For the LORD is a God of justice. Blessed are all who wait for him." NIV

Jeremiah knew. Out of his lament (Lamentations 3:22) comes this crowning moment: "It is of the LORD's mercies that we are not consumed, because his compassions fail not."

Micah joins the procession in 7:19: "He will turn again, he will have compassion upon us; he will subdue our iniquities; and thou wilt cast all their sins into the depths of the sea."

Hosea, charged to live out the nature of the Name with his whoring wife Gomer, passionately declares the heart of God: "How can I give you up, Ephraim? How can I hand you over, Israel? How can I treat you like Admah? How can I make you like Zeboim? My heart is changed within me; all my compassion is aroused." Hosea 11:8 NIV
The knowing, if not the living, went on.

Jonah Knew

Jonah certainly knew what God was like and it got him into trouble. Jonah was a racist of the first order. He hated the city of Nineveh. No city had been crueler to Israel. No city could surpass it in wickedness. No city would he like to be rid of more than that one. Gladly would he see it go down in flames.

So, God says, "Jonah, you are my man. I have a message that will fit your attitude perfectly. I, too, hate Nineveh. Go and tell them that I am going to destroy them in forty days because of their sin." You would think that Jonah would rise and race to Nineveh energized by the glee of his message, but, no, he takes another course. Jonah seeks to flee Nineveh and hide from God. However, if you are going to run from God, don't hide in his living room. God found Jonah; the men of the ship found Jonah; the great fish found Jonah; and then Jonah found himself.

After a whalesize seashore vomit, Jonah scurries to Nineveh fully convinced that preaching to them was the thing to do. At least he still has a great message: destruction. I can see the gleam in his eye as he delivers the scathing ultimatum, the ultimatum that offered no recourse—forty days and you will be destroyed!

Something must have nagged Jonah, tugged at his insides, whispered in his ear as he delivered his tirades. He knew a secret about his God and that secret was going to ruin things for him. He just knew it!

Day forty rolls around and Jonah moves safely outside the city to watch the fireworks. He had waited for this moment most of his life. He felt privileged to be able to be a part of this great destructive scene. One minor hitch had developed, but surely that would not stay the great declaration of God. So, the city had repented.

What difference should that make? Who really knows about death-bed conversions, anyway? The backlog of evil behind their cracking dam was enough to destroy generations miles down the stream. What was about to happen, he thought, was only right.

He waited, shifting about to improve his view, and waited and waited. Nothing happened. "Perhaps my calendar is off. Maybe I have miscounted. Maybe I should wait another day. This cannot be! My license as a prophet will be revoked. My hatred is too intense to be wasted." Because his eyes were focused on the hope of destruction he failed to notice the little cloud of gloom that maneuvered to a good resting spot over his head. The pity party had begun. Jonah deserved this "pout." He had earned it.

Unreturned love has driven the pens of songwriters for centuries, but the song being sung on this day for Jonah was of unfulfilled vengeance. It was a nasty melody but it was tops on his hit parade.

In His Name, but Not In His Nature

Nineveh later backslid and was destroyed. Perhaps Jonah, who brought the revival that converted a whole city, was also the source of its downfall. I can see him slumped in his favorite pouting position. Life and activity proceed. Passing feet scuffle the road.

"Dad, who is that man over there?"
"That is the pastor, son."
"Why is he pouting? What's wrong with him?"
"He is angry, son."
"Why, Dad?"
"Because we are still alive."
"Oh."

And why shouldn't Jonah be there. He had expressed himself to God in no uncertain terms in that great paradoxical opening to Jonah 4:

> But Jonah was greatly displeased and became angry. He prayed to the LORD, "O LORD [YHWH], is this not what I said when I was still at home? That is why I was so quick to flee to Tarshish. I knew that you are a gracious and compassionate God, slow to anger and abounding in love, a God who relents from sending calamity." NIV

The secret was out. God was God and Jonah was Jonah. *Jonah came in God's name but not in his nature.* Jonah condemns and God forgives. Jonah pouts and God rejoices. Jonah destroys and God saves. The nature of God survives today. So does the nature of Jonah.

Joel and Nehemiah Knew

In the midst of the earth-rending destruction of Joel 2, a ray of hope beams through the centuries from the mirror of Moses on the top of that mountain and lands at the feet of Israel. Joel records:

> Therefore also now, saith the LORD,
> turn ye even to me with all your heart, and
> with fasting, and with weeping, and with
> mourning: And rend your heart, and not
> your garments, and turn unto the LORD
> your God: *for he is gracious and merciful,*
> *slow to anger, and of great kindness,* and re-
> penteth him of the evil. Joel 2:12,13 (My em-
> phasis)

The beam of God's grace and nature bounces at that spot and lands again in Acts 2 carrying with it God's loving fulfillment of his nature to a people who have repented or who need to:

> And it shall come to pass afterward,
> that I will pour out my spirit upon all flesh;
> and your sons and your daughters shall
> prophesy, your old men shall dream
> dreams, your young men shall see visions:
> And also upon the servants and upon the
> handmaids in those days will I pour out my
> spirit. Joel 2:28,29 see Acts 2:17-21

One last powerful statement occurs that Luke quotes in Acts. He states, "And everyone who calls on the name of the Lord will be saved;..." (Joel 2:32) It is not he who lives well or achieves much or fulfills any of the expectations we have for religious people who will be saved. No, it is he who calls on the name of the Lord. And his Name? Gracious, compassionate, slow to anger.... It is only God, never us, only God who saves. We are objects of his grace.

Just hours before the Old Testament pages are closed, we see the Grace/Glory/Name of God being used again by Nehemiah. Jerusalem, God's city had been overrun, its gates and walls destroyed, its people living in fear and subservience beneath corrupt leaders. Nehemiah, a man of stature, comes under the authority of the king and guides the rebuilding of the walls. The job complete, attention now turns to the spiritual condition of the people. Ezra reads the Law. The people repent and worship and in the middle of their moment of worship, Nehemiah, in his book, expresses a prayer that can come only from an understanding of the heart of God (My emphasis):

> ...Blessed be your glorious name, and may it be exalted above all blessing and praise. 9:5
> You are the LORD God, who chose Abraham....
> You found his heart faithful to you, and you made a covenant with him.... 9:7,8
> But they, our forefathers, became arrogant and stiff-necked, and did not obey your commands... 9:16
> But you are a forgiving God, gracious and compassionate, slow to anger and abounding in love. *Therefore you did not desert them, ...9:17*
> But they were disobedient and rebelled against you; they put your law behind their backs. They killed your prophets,..... 9:26
> And when they cried out to you again, you heard from heaven, and in *your com-*

passion you delivered them time after time.
9:28
    But in your great mercy you did not put an end to them or abandon them, **for you are a gracious and merciful God.** 9:31 NIV

Nehemiah offers no excuse for the people. Their life style was in direct contrast with the nature of their God and with his commandments. Nothing justified their wicked actions. Only one response is appropriate—sackcloth and ashes and confession. In the midst of confession, in the collecting pond of humility, Nehemiah remembers, "But you are a forgiving God, gracious and compassionate, slow to anger and abounding in love." Case opened, testimony taken, guilty as accused, forgiven as declared, case closed. Nehemiah exits in a blaze of glory asking only, "Remember me with favor, O my God."

Remember Me with Favor

Four hundred years is a long time to wait to see if God's description of himself is accurate. The valley of mankind stretches long across history begging for help, a deliverer, a Messiah, an "anointed one." Will he come? Is YHWH touchable? Can he be seen? Will the desert blossom? Will every mountain be brought low? Will every valley be exalted?

Shortly we will leave the desolate, violent days of the Old Testament and climb the wall to the New Testament to see what kind of new Garden of Eden God has planted for us traveling Adams, but first we must look at additional evidence of his nature expressed in the Covenants.

The Covenants

God seems to like contracts, he keeps signing so many of them. Interestingly enough, he keeps signing contracts that bind him to certain action and then leaves the requirements for us blank with no signature necessary.

The first of these contracts clearly stated is:

> And it shall come to pass, when I bring a cloud over the earth, that the bow shall be seen in the cloud: And I will remember my covenant, which is between me and you and every living creature of all flesh; and the waters shall no more become a flood to destroy all flesh. And the bow shall be in the cloud; and I will look upon it, that I may remember the everlasting covenant between God and every living creature of all flesh that is upon the earth. And God said unto Noah, "This is the token of the covenant, which I have established between me and all flesh that is upon the earth." Genesis 9:14-17

The earth, now cleansed from the cancerous wickedness that possessed it, will find the seed of wickedness only briefly dormant in the hearts of the passengers on the Ark. Regardless, God signs a covenant stating that he will never again destroy the earth by water and the signature will be a very colorful one that he and all earthlings would be able to observe together—the rainbow.

Here again we see the nature of God shining through. He desires the best for creation and is committed to the contract whether creation gives proper response or not. Nothing Noah or anyone else did or ever will do could keep God from keeping this unilateral covenant.

The covenant with Noah was not the only unilateral covenant God signed. Just three chapters (but many years) later, a remarkable promise is made to a man named Abraham for reasons that would escape anyone looking for worldly logic.

> And I will make of thee a great nation, and I will bless thee, and make thy name great; and thou shalt be a blessing:
> And I will bless them that bless thee, and curse him that curseth thee: and in thee shall all families of the earth be blessed. Genesis 12:2,3

Wham! Just like that, Abraham has a contract with God that exceeds anything anyone could ever want. What did Abraham do to deserve it? Apparently nothing! Indeed, he might have been a pagan worshiper of idols with no claim on anything but the wrath of God. Yet into his life comes this surprising encounter whose details are hinted at when Jesus states in John 8:56, "Your father Abraham rejoiced at the thought of seeing my day; he saw it and was glad."

But why Abraham? Sheer, sovereign grace! And what did he see that caused him literally to leap for joy? Since he saw the day of Jesus, he must have been given insight into the nature of God and his ultimate redemption of mankind. Remember that Abraham as a man was no different from any of us. He was beset with sin, anxiety, difficulties. The need for life-changing redemption is not unique to modern society.

So, when Abraham was given a vision in his encounter with God of his grace and redemption, it was enough to move him to leave his household to become a dreaming wanderer going who-knows-where. The grace of God was powerful enough even then to drive a man to irrational action, including the willingness later to sacrifice his own son at the command of a grace-natured God. When you have seen the nature and redemption of God you *know* that everything will work out best, regardless of how it seems on the surface.

Caught in this hope dream of how God is, Abraham commits another irrational act—he lets his nephew Lot have the first choice (thus the better choice—Lot was no dummy) of pasture land even though this flew in the face of traditions that let the elder choose first. It appears that Abraham was learning to serve others just like the God who had blessed him. Congratulations, Abraham.

Of course, we must delete the incredible failures of Abraham, such as his lying about Sarah twice in order to save his own neck. We must delete them, that is, unless we also believe in the overwhelming grace of God who places his favor on us for his own sake and not as a reward for our righteousness. God had pulled the curtains of time and let Abraham see the day of Jesus. The report in John 8:56 indicates that Abraham was beside himself with joy at the vision of the future coming of Jesus.

But Abraham believed God (Genesis 15:6) and that was all God needed to get carried away again with new contracts:

Abraham is credited with righteousness because he believed!

Abraham is promised a son at his senior, senior citizen age!

Abraham is given victory over all his enemies!

Abraham is introduced to and blessed by Melchizedek, founder of the priestly order to whom Christ belonged!

Promise is given that Abraham will become the father of many nations with people outnumbering the sands of the sea, and his name is appropriately changed from Abram to Abraham.

Abraham is promised prosperity.

God goes through an ancient covenant ceremony with Abraham to prove his intentions. (Genesis 15:17,18) In this ritual, the parties to a contract were to pass between the split carcasses of a sacrifice as a visible signature to their promise. But now behold the one-sided grace of

God: *only God passed between the carcasses, which means only God signed the contract! Amazing grace.*

God promises Abraham a land of his own for his people.

All this was given to Abraham only because God chose to do so. The only thing Abraham did that was worthy was to believe.

Fulfillment of this contract continues through the centuries. God has blessed Abraham and his children of the Spirit and of the flesh and also God has blessed the world through Abraham and his seed. As Don Richardson has developed in his book **Eternity in Their Hearts**, pick any hero or heroine of your choice in the Old Testament and you will find them at some point being beneficial to others, even their enemies at times. Certainly, the ultimate fulfillment has been in Jesus and in the blessing that is distributed through those who follow him, but an interesting controversy has arisen of late about the nature of the covenant.

Recently, some religious people applied the blessing passages of Abraham into our physical situation today. They claim that the financial and physical prosperity promised to Abraham is not only available but mandatory in our Christian walk. Those who teach that our faith must produce prosperity claim that curses and hindrances to Old Testament blessing are lifted or defeated in Jesus. Then they say we must live in opulence as the children of kings of this world live. This opulence and health, they believe, is achieved through exercise of the right kind of faith or through repeating or confessing the scripture in the right way.

Of course, not everyone accepts this practice as a legitimate understanding of faith or proper use of scripture. A remarkable passage in the New Testament specifically renews the Abrahamic covenant of Genesis 12 and refutes their case. But first let us approach from another direction a refutation of the physical interpretation that such wealth teachers use for our day.

As shown in *The Jesus Style* and as seen in the Sinai revelation, the very nature of God is to be others-centered and unselfish. Jesus, king of kings, did not come to be served but to serve and give himself away. The very cornerstone of following him is grounded in denying ourselves and giving our lives away. (Matthew 16:24,25) Thus, two logical conclusions can quickly come from our understanding of this nature of Jesus.

First, we must not in any way take our understanding of kingship from the kings of this world. Jesus plainly stated that his kingdom was not of this world, else his followers would fight for him. So, if we are to maintain that we must live like "king's kids," the only king to whom we must relate is Jesus, the king who expressed his kingship only through the act of serving. Jetsetting and palaces must be replaced in our thinking with donkeys and mangers if we would be children of our king.

Second, the very nature of prosperity-oriented faith is that we might *gain for ourselves*. Such a life style is tailor-made for self-centeredness and is fueled by the pride of life and the lust of the eyes. Interestingly enough, this particular type of outlook gains its greatest foothold among those who are already prosperous and have bought into a more gain-oriented style of life. This way of thinking merely undergirds the culture and greed of mankind.

I have seen such teaching planted and blossom for a short time in poorer areas of the third world as a people begin to hope that perhaps they can tie in to whatever made the white man prosper. Soon they abandon the teaching after realizing that it basically doesn't work. Next, as they think it through, they realize that the resulting difficulties of such a prosperity belief structure requires damaging reinterpretation of God and scripture. Finally, candidness forces them to observe that new churches formed around prosperity doctrine feed on already established churches severely dividing the body of Christ rather than enlarging it.

Now, we look to the New Testament to see how they understood the continuation of God's contract with Abraham and his children. Luke gets to the specifics in Acts:

> And you are heirs of the prophets and of the covenant God made with your fathers. He said to Abraham, "Through your offspring all peoples on earth will be blessed." When God raised up his servant, he sent him first to you to bless you by turning each of you from your wicked ways. Acts 3:24,25 NIV

Obviously, the fulfillment of the Abrahamic blessing to us is that Jesus would come and turn us from our wicked ways. If financial prosperity had been the focal point, surely the writer would have signaled it at this point, especially to the baby church now facing persecution and the loss of all possessions. But Luke ignored that teaching. We have no indication he even knew of it or considered it. But Luke is not alone in his understanding of the role of Jesus in this contract. Let us listen to Paul in his letter to Ephesus: (My emphasis)

> Praise be to the God and Father of our Lord Jesus Christ, who has **blessed us in the heavenly realms with every spiritual blessing in Christ.** 1:3
> And you also were included in Christ when you heard the word of truth, the gospel of your salvation. Having believed, you were marked in him with a seal, **the promised Holy Spirit, who is a deposit guaranteeing our inheritance** until the redemption of those who are God's possession—to the praise of his glory. 13,14 NIV

So, here again, the understanding that Jesus and the redemption and spiritual blessing we have in him are the fulfillment of the facets of the Abrahamic contract. We are even sealed and guaranteed by the Holy Spirit that at the final moment of redemption, our inheritance will be made complete. Again, nothing financial is even hinted. In the greatness and eloquence with which Paul describes our relationship with

Christ in Ephesians, it seems almost sacrilegious to let the thought of Caesar's realm enter.

Luke details the other side of the covenant renewal quoted earlier: "Through your offspring all peoples on earth will be blessed." (Acts 3:25 NIV) Amazing that this is the only part of the covenant that would be quoted. Why? Obviously, this is the only part that needs to be quoted. Since Jesus has fulfilled the part of blessing us, it remains only that we should now continue in his nature and bless the rest of the world.

So God still keeps his contract—he blesses us and then others through us. What a joy to know him and make him known.

THE FATHER STYLE

Part Four

THE ROCK

A Set of Beliefs

In this chapter reside the beliefs and understandings that fueled the first part of the book. Here are the traits of Jesus that drove me to search out the nature of the Father in a new way, then the discoveries that drove me back to the New Testament to see Jesus anew.

This chapter could just as easily have been the introduction, but for the sake of a better reflection, let us now look at the sets of information or beliefs and review the background to bridge our theme into the New Testament.

Belief #1

The Nature of Jesus is summed up in his "Greatest in the Kingdom" teachings in the Gospels and Paul's Philippians 2:5-11 passage. (See **The Jesus Style** by Gayle D. Erwin.) Those traits of his nature are:

1. Servant

Slave would be a better word. Jesus freed others to become all they were created to be. He was the one others-centered person in history.

2. Not lord it over others

In contrast to the leaders of the kingdom of the world (i.e, the Gentiles), Jesus did not lord it over others nor did he get his understanding of who he was by how many people he was *over*.

3. Example

In contrast to the leaders of the kingdom of religion (i.e., teachers of the Law who sat in the seat of Moses), Jesus practiced what he preached. The only valid form of leadership in the kingdom of God is leadership by example.

4. Humble

Jesus lived a life of absolute honesty about himself. He walked without pretense, without hypocrisy. Humility is not a mincing self-negation, but an open honesty about oneself. We arrive at humility by way of confession—telling the truth about ourselves.

5. As a child

Jesus taught by example the simple, un-threatening, innocent-faith approach of childlikeness. No one was ever afraid of him in spite of his awesome power. He walked as a lamb among wolves and sent his followers out in the same way.

6. As the younger

The younger brother was all-but-left-out in the financial stream of inheritance in those mid-Eastern countries. The elder brother—receiver of the "birthright"—was the blessed one, the beneficiary of tradition. On the other hand, for the younger brother the system of the world was not on his side. When Jesus said for us to be as the younger, he was calling us to a life that accepts its disadvantaged, temporary status. This was a call from Jesus for us to be pilgrims passing through this world, recognizing that here "we have no enduring city."

7. As the last

Actively putting other people first. This comes out of love for people, not out of desire to be noticed as *last*.

8. As the least

Virtually identical to being *as the last*, being least is the logical product of putting others first. Sometimes going first when an undesirable job must be done is the same as being least.

The traits listed above are taken from Jesus' own teachings about himself in the "greatest in the kingdom" series in the Gospels. The following six traits are gleaned from the "mind of Christ" passage in Philippians 2:5-11.

9. Used no physical force on people

With all his power, Jesus could have forced us to do anything he wanted us to do, but he refused to violate anyone or to destroy any person's ability to choose.

10. Was not driven by blind ambition

Jesus never employed ungodly methods though his heavenly goal would have been an excellent excuse for doing so. He came to redeem people, not run over them.

11. Made himself of no reputation

Rather than join the ranks of the elite and uphold some "royal" image, Jesus made himself of no reputation so he would be approachable to all people. Sinners were comfortable in his presence.

12. Completely human

Jesus operated as a Spirit-filled human. He was fully God and fully man. Consequently, he knows mankind and the human condition—how "dusty" we are. He was "tempted in all points like we are."

13. Obedient

Jesus never varied from revealing the traits and will of the Father. His food (meat) was to "do the will of him who sent me." He told us that he only did what he saw the Father do and only said what he heard the Father say.

14. Gave up his life
Death is the ultimate test of our servanthood. Jesus never tried to save his life and thus subvert the walk of redemption. He was faithful to the cross.

Belief #2

Since Jesus was like the Father, then these traits would also be traits of the Father. If these are the traits of the Father, he who changes not would surely have been trying to reveal himself this way in the Old Testament.

Belief #3

Confirmation of matching natures of Jesus and the Father occur in Exodus 34 as God reveals the meaning of his name to Moses. The traits of that revelation are:

1. **Compassionate**
2. **Gracious or merciful**
3. **Slow to anger**
4. **Abounding in love**
5. **Abounding in faithfulness**
6. **Maintaining love to thousands**
7. **Forgiving wickedness**
8. **Forgiving rebellion**

9. **Forgiving sin**
10. **Holding man accountable**

Belief #4

When Moses asked to see the Glory of God, the responding revelation attached the meaning of his Name to the revelation of his Glory so they would be understood as the same. In other words, Name=Glory or His Name/Nature and His Glory are the same.

Belief #5

The Father gave Jesus his own Name and Glory (as we will see in this chapter), which solves some old theological problems (i.e., baptism) and provides exciting new understanding of prayer and Christian activity.

The Bridge

Studying the Nature of Jesus gives us a key that helps unlock the Old Testament, and now, within the room of the Nature of the Father, we find another key that returns us to the New Testament ready to discover Jesus as we never have before.

John seems to know where the door to the secret room is located: "We have seen his glory, the glory of the one and only Son, who came from the Father, full of grace and truth." (John 1:14)

Immediately we remember the "compassion and grace and abounding truth" in the nature of the Father and can safely conclude that one has proceeded from the other. Now we have genetic evidence.

John continues to give us another clue: "From the fullness of his grace we have all received one blessing after another." (John 1:16) This grace is important to John. He does not dwell on the recurrent pulpit theme that God has now sent his son to judge or get even with us. No, John uses words like "creation, light, life, children of God, glory, grace, truth." These qualities have to be the result of some incredible *Good* exploding on the scene.

Just so we won't get the situation mixed up and make any wrong conclusions, John separates the two testaments clearly and then describes the bridge with these next words: "For the law was given through Moses; grace and truth came through Jesus Christ." (John 1:17) The steadily deteriorating human race, already an object of God's mercy, now is going to hear the Word straight from its origin. Now, from the mouth of God himself, not hearsay from Moses, they will know that grace abounds, that God has ushered in the season of his favor. Jesus is, indeed, the bridge that brings the Father close enough for us to touch. Jesus is the bridge.

Glory Plus

Before we look at the main treasures, how does Paul see this mixture of the Glory and the Name? He tweaks our interest with an obscure but powerful progression in 2 Corinthians 3:7-18. (My emphasis)

> Now if the ministry that brought **death**, which was engraved in letters on stone, came with glory, so that the Israelites could not look steadily at the face of Moses because of its glory, fading though it was, will not the ministry of the Spirit be even more **glorious**? If the ministry that condemns men is glorious, how much more **glorious** is the ministry that brings righteousness! For what was glorious has no glory now in comparison with the surpassing glory. And if what was fading away came with glory, how much greater is the glory of that which lasts. 7-11 NIV

The Apostle Paul loved to build logical cases and to present evidence in a way that made the resolution seem like fireworks. In this case, one cannot miss the comparison being made. We are being pointed toward something so much better that it is almost impossible to describe. He is building the dramatic moment—increasing our expectancy beyond bounds. He begins Verse 7 with "Now" and rewards us in Verse 12 with "Therefore." (Emphases and parenthetical comments are mine.)

> Therefore, since we have such a hope, [that we have a greater, surpassing glory that

does not fade away] *we are very bold. We are not like Moses, who would put a veil [*similar to the concept of "masks." *Hiding has existed since the fall of mankind.] *over his face to keep the Israelites from gazing at it while the radiance was fading away.* 12,13 NIV

How sad that their leader was fading away or "losing out with God." We hate to see our heroes weaken. I can feel the excitement of the Israelites as they see the face of Moses after his encounter with God. In the middle of a desert, you need all the encouragement you can get. I can hear the conversation in my imagination:

"That's our leader, man."

"Yeah. Can you see his face?"

"I sure can! Look at that shine. He's been with God!"

"Yeah. What else can that mean?"

Soon the chants of the excited crowd would begin. "Moses! Moses! Moses!..." It must have been a heady moment. But the next day mutes the response just a little.

"There's our leader again."

"Yeah. The man who has been with God."

"Look at his face. It radiates."

"True, but not quite as bright as yesterday."

"Maybe, but it is still OK."

"Moses! Moses! Moses!..."

This could have political impact. The last thing these people need to think is that God is departing from their leader. We will deny such a possibility as long as we can. No leader of such a people could afford to admit such a dangerous situation nor could the people permit themselves to accept it. One more day and the solution could only be obvious.

"There he is. That's Moses, our great leader."

"Sure is. The man who has been with God."

"Yes, it is easy to tell. Just look at his face."

"I am. It is impressive, but dimmer than it was. I wonder what is wrong."

"I don't know. Maybe there is sin in his life. Maybe he is not as close to God as he was. Maybe God is angry with him. Who knows?"

"Yeah. Who knows?"

Some things threaten a leader too much. If Moses had been one of the crowd, it would have been embarrassing enough but not quite as threatening. As a leader, certain appearances were to be maintained. Of course, he had options. Disappear from view for a while. Refuse to hold press conferences. Speak only through other officials. Go back up on the mountain to see if the old glow would return. Tell the people a fading face is a sign of maturity. Tell the people to look at their own faces and leave Moses alone. Tell the people that his face is still brighter than anyone else's and certainly brighter than Pharaoh's face. Throw anyone in jail who talks about faces.

The options were many, but only one was direct and easy—hide. So he did. The veil covered his face. The gaze was averted.

There is a certain irony here. A veiled face is as unusual as a bright one. Certainly it would be cause for gazing. Surely the question would be asked, "Who is the man with the veil over his face and why would he be wearing it?" But, Moses, like all humanity, assumes it is better to hide. Now, the hidden Moses is reduced to the same state as everyone else—no glow. That is more comforting to everyone than watching the glow fade away.

But, *we are not like Moses.*

Paul continues with the examination of this veil, so symbolic of so many things, and applies it to the spiritual sight of Israel.

> But their minds were made dull, for to this day the same veil remains when the old covenant is read. It has not been removed, because **only in Christ** *is it taken away. Even to this day when Moses is read, a veil covers their hearts. But whenever anyone turns to the Lord, the veil is taken away. vs. 14-16* NIV

The veil, symbol of our hiding. The veil, that barrier between us and the Holy of Holies—the place where his Name is and where his mercy dwells. The veil, symbol of our darkness and dullness. The veil, fearful wall of both death and glory.

Until Jesus.

Jesus walked behind that veil carrying all the sins the world had ever committed and ever would commit. That was a violation unacceptable to the law. The high priest in the Temple dared to go only once a year into that awesome place behind the curtain. Even then he must go in with a sinless life or he would be struck dead—such a paradox—in the presence of the Mercy Seat. Flesh, the maggot infested store-house of sin, simply could not behold his glory. Terror walked with the priest who was chosen to sprinkle the blood on the Mercy Seat that one time of the year. Would he be able to live sinlessly for a year? For a month? For a day?

What thoughts invaded the priest's mind as he watched them sew the bells to the bottom of his skirt—the decoration whose silence signaled death. Apprehension surely gripped him as other priests tied a rope around his ankle so at least they could retrieve his body should the sound cease. He knew the terror of the Lord.

Until Jesus.

No bell or rope existed to preserve the sin-laden sinless one. Jesus entered the Holiest Place and there he died. There was no tug of rescue from his closest followers, only a bor-rowed tomb from a secret friend. What a failure. What a relief for the Sanhedrin. No more of this pandering to the poor and blaspheming the name of their God. What a relief to Rome. Maybe now, this crowd of poor people will settle down to peaceful living.

Until...some cosmic lightening bolt came from Heaven and the veil, that separated man-kind from access to his mercy in the Temple, was split from top to bottom. Aha, from top to bottom. It could not have been the work of some man. Only Heaven could rip it from that direc-tion. (Mark 15:38) "Only in Christ is it taken away."

Do you know what happened next? Do you know what the keepers of that temple did? They sewed the veil back up! Nothing could be sadder than that.

Even today, we attempt to sew the veil back together—to limit access to his mercy. For some reason we consistently corrupt the simplicity of access to God by developing complicated formulas that supposedly make us finally acceptable for fellowship with God. Whole denominations and other religious organizations have been formed around the concept, "In order to reach God, you must do these things."

I have heard teaching that demanded that we restore our worship styles to a "Davidic" form with stages of worship built around the design of the Tabernacle/Temple. The concept of that teaching is that as we sing increasingly intimate songs of worship, we move from "outer court" to "inner court" of closeness to God until, finally, we have reached the point of emotion and relationship with God that he will permit us to enter the "Holy of Holies." I agree with their hearts and their goal and value any attempt to worship the true and living God, but the Old Testament formulaic demand is simply trying to sew the veil back together. While others may think they are still in the outer court of singing, I am already in the Holy of Holies. Jesus has already granted me access and I refuse to be deterred from his presence. The veil has been removed. Don't put it back!

Also, when Jesus in John 4 told the Samaritan woman that worship would no longer be associated with a place, but would be acceptable only in spirit and truth, he permanently squelched any attempts to restore worship to binding patterns.

Just so we cannot possibly misunderstand, Paul crowns his argument with statements that leave us breathless in the throne-room. Keep in mind our belief that the Name and the Glory of God are tied together and they both speak of his revealed nature. (My emphasis)

> Now the Lord is the Spirit, and where the Spirit of the Lord is, there is freedom. And we, who with **unveiled faces** all reflect the Lord's glory, are being transformed into his likeness with **ever-increasing glory**, which comes from the Lord, who is the Spirit. 17,18 NIV

We know, from what we have just read, that we are not like Moses. We know that we have a greater glory that will not fade. We know that we can be very bold. So, just what do these verses mean? Let me explain with a story.

I was once part of a group of ministers who would meet every six weeks or so and spend most of a day together for fellowship and growth. At one meeting, after we had said hello to each other, one of the men began to weep and ask for our help. He said, "Fellows, I have had a problem in my life for ten years, now, and it is no better today than it was ten years ago. I thought I had prayed the right prayers and done the right things, but it is no better today. Is there any hope for me? Can you help me?" We all nodded our identification with him as he spoke.

For some reason, everyone turned and looked at me. "Gayle, how do you handle something like this?"

"Men, I have found that I am powerless to change myself. The more I try, the more I see that I can't. I have found that, rather than improve myself, my practice only makes permanent my weaknesses. The problems I have are like dragons hidden in a cave and when I decide to tackle one of them, that very decision is like throwing meat to him to make him stronger for the fight. For example, if I decide to do something about my weight, suddenly all the world turns into food!

"The only thing I have found that produces any good change in me is found in 2 Corinthians 3:18. When I face my failure, my sin, I pull the veil aside and show my face to the Lord and say, 'Here I am, Lord. I need your help.' I have learned to do this immediately, like immediate confession, and keep myself exposed to the Lord by pulling the veil aside. Then, I discover that he does the changing."

The Great God-Change

Can you see what is happening in this passage? We expose ourselves to God (confess?); we bare our hearts to him, or remove the veil from our faces; God shines his Glory (grace, compassion, forgiveness) on us; and we reflect God's work in us to others. What an incredible promise! Our openness and confession does not move God to zap us or to bring about his judgment. No. Instead, he shines his grace upon us and produces another almost-unbelievable result.

In addition to the spotlight of his grace, we find that we "are being changed." Did you hear that? This is a passive statement. That means that *we* are not doing the changing, it is *happening to us*. God is doing the changing. That way, he will be sure to get the glory for the change. All we can do is to receive his glory and reflect.

But the story is still not over. Not only do we have the spotlight of his grace shined upon us, and not only do we find ourselves being changed, but we know what we are being changed into—his likeness. Too much! Sometimes I resist change, because the change does not seem to be for the better. Moses must have resisted and resented his change because it definitely was a reduction from a state of glory. But we know the destiny of our change. We are being changed into the likeness of Christ. Now I know why God has to do the work. I could never accomplish this task within myself.

And the destiny? What a marvelous goal. We remove the veil—he makes us like Christ. Who else would you want to be like? What other goal would you prefer? He doesn't just agree to make us better or not as bad. Instead, God offers us the likeness of his Son. And what did we have to do to get this? Only rip the veil aside. Only reveal ourselves to God.

"But," you say, "there must be something I must do." There you go sewing the veil back up.

"But, this is cheap grace." There you go sewing the veil back up.

"I don't want anything free. I'll earn it." There you go sewing the veil back up.

"I'll turn over a new leaf. I'll change my ways." There you go sewing the veil back up.

The Cart with Pull

I have a weakness that I hesitate to reveal to you, but it is true and it illustrates my point, so here goes...*chocolate-covered raisins.* Sometimes, when my wife sends me to the grocery store for milk, I walk into the store and grab one of the carts. Now, I know where the milk is. It is a straight shot to the back of the store. But there is something about the cart that keeps pulling me toward a certain aisle.

Sure enough, I find myself in that aisle where the chocolate-covered raisins are. I try to pretend that I am only traveling down this aisle. I look furtively around, but my gaze locks on to those luscious things. I decide to speak to them.

"I don't need you. I have you conquered. That's why I came down this aisle. I just wanted to show you how conquered you are. So, there!" And I head on to the milk.

I get the milk and put it in my cart. Now, the check-out counter is a straight shot from the milk to the front of the store, but there is something about that cart that keeps pulling me, and I find myself going back up that aisle. Once again, I am there beside those delectable, delicious...things. I speak again.

"See, I told you that I don't need you. I've got you conquered. That's why I came back up this aisle, just to show you how conquered you are. In fact, I am going to show you just how conquered you are. I am going to buy you and not eat you!" I put the package in my cart and go through the check-out.

When I get home, my wife asks me, "What's this?" I tell her not to worry, I know what I am doing. So I sit down and look at them. I decide to speak to them again.

"See, I've got you conquered. I've passed by you, bought you and brought you home. I don't need you. I am your master. In fact, I am going to show you just how conquered you are; I am going to open you and eat only one!"

When I finish the package, I am sick and I hate myself. I sit and write new resolutions. I adopt a guilty look. For the next three times that I go to the grocery store, I don't even go down that aisle. Then, on the fourth visit....

Does this sound familiar to you? Substitute anything you want for the chocolate-covered raisins. What can we do? Is there any hope? The only thing we can do, the only hope we have is in Christ. We must keep the veil away from our faces. How often can we do that? However often we need to!

We don't come boldly before the throne of grace to show off our accomplishments. We come boldly before the throne of grace to get help. (Hebrews 4:16)

But the story is not over yet. We are changed with "ever-increasing glory." In other words, there is not some sudden burst of God's grace followed only by small streams and trickles. No. As we grow more like him, we also receive more of his grace.

When I was younger, I was confident that I would be able to take life by the horns and make it mine. I was sure that I would have most of my problems solved by the time I was forty and be in a state of diminishing need of grace. Was I ever surprised. The older I get, the more aware and honest about myself I become. The more honest I am, the more I know I need his grace— more now than ever. God knows that, so he supplies "ever-increasing glory." God does not tire of me nor decrease my favor, he keeps enlarging the pipeline.

So, we are not like Moses. Moses had seen the Glory and, now, all he could do was fade away. We, too, have seen his Glory and all we can do is "ever-increase." Glory!

But the story is not over yet. Once we boldly but humbly receive his grace, a great "therefore" awaits us. "Therefore" meaning because of what has happened, a natural succession of revelation is pending—another awesome moment. We will now examine a passage that leads us further into his grace.

Clay Meets Gold

If our own personal situations are so hopeless, as we saw in the prior chapter; if all changing must be done by God and not ourselves, our chance to be profitably used in the kingdom of God seems rather poor. Fortunately, that is not so. We continue into 2 Corinthians 4 and hear these phenomenal opening words:

> Therefore, since through God's mercy we have this ministry, we do not lose heart.
> NIV

Insight! Just as our improvement is a product of his mercy, so our participation in any sort of ministry is also a product of his mercy. Any honest person considers himself unlikely ever to be used for divine purposes. Left to myself, I am uncontrollably greedy. The only difference between myself and the criminal who gains by gun is style.

So, how in the world could I even have a ministry? Mercy. Only mercy.

"But wait! Isn't it obvious from watching television that ministry is the logical product of someone who is handsome, articulate, talented and charismatic?" No, the only *logical* product of those traits is pride. Ministry, any ministry, is allowed because of God's mercy. It takes extra mercy to trust someone with those naturally outstanding traits with any kind of ministry.

"But, wait again. Ministry costs money. Every ministry must have someone who knows how to raise money. That is just the way the world works. So, if you know how to get the bills paid, that qualifies you for ministry." Sorry. Greed cannot be sanctified and renamed "fundraising." Remember, the difference between tears and guns is only style. "Seeking first the kingdom of God" might qualify you to "have all these other things added to you," but mercy, by definition, excludes all other qualifications for ministry.

"But, wait once more. We call our pastor 'Reverend.' That has to mean some sort of higher quality in him. Also, he moves in more elite spiritual circles, wears better clothes, drives better cars and has special parking places. When we chose him to be pastor, we didn't look for some wimp. We wanted class, 'ministerial' class. There must be a quality difference."

Enough! Mercy is not being judged here, our standards and practices are. Not one single thing we have mentioned so far is, in any way, listed (or even hinted) as part of ministry. If a lot of legend and a handful of clues are true, the Apostle Paul had squinty, weak eyes, a hunched back; he was short and spoke with a squeaky, high-pitched grating voice. Imagine that kind of person and then imagine whether you would want him as your pastor. So, let Paul change the world. Let Paul shape theology for 2000 years.

But, keep him away from our churches, because he lacks "ministerial" quality. All he has is...well...mercy.

Depression Therapy

"What did I do to deserve this?" is seldom a positive statement. Just when things seem to be getting stable, disaster strikes and life crumbles once again. I knew of one pastor who would be so discouraged every Monday morning that he would drive by the city-limit sign just to practice leaving.

We teach and we teach. They don't hear and they don't hear. We practice and we practice. They ignore and ignore. We preach and we preach and they sin and they sin. "Forget it," we say. "I don't deserve this kind of treatment." Gather round, ye Words of Distress. Arise, Mope. Enter, Raven of "Nevermore."

Whoa! Paul said, "We do not lose heart." In other words, "We don't get discouraged." Why? Because we have this ministry by sheer mercy anyway. Frankly, if we were terribly mistreated, it would be better than we deserved. If only two people ever listened to us, it would be more than we deserved.

Since mercy provides the ministry, mercy delivers the results. When I truly understand that concept, no reason remains to lose heart. We become joyously obedient to our own heavenly vision and not miserable reactors to "the mess we are in." Mercy wins again.

Finally, the Face

We observed in Exodus that Moses could not bear to see the face of God. That would be too much for him. So, God permits only a glimpse of his back. His face remains hidden, secret, mysterious. Will it always be withheld? Will we ever see?

We also learned that the definition of his Name and revelation of his Glory were the same. His very nature is wrapped together in his Name and Glory. That brings us to the next scripture— a spiritual Mount Everest peak.

> For God, who said, "Let light shine out of darkness," made his light shine in our hearts to give us the light of the knowledge of the glory of God in the face of Christ.
> 2 Corinthians 4:6 NIV

At last, after Jesus' death and resurrection we reach the ultimate Sinai. Now, God walks straight toward us. No hand need hide us from him. Now his hand holds us. We look for his face and discover it is there. It smiles at us. The face is Jesus. Now we see God face to face.

Wait a minute. Wouldn't seeing his face kill you? Well, somebody had to die for us to see him. Someone walked sin-laden behind the veil and was struck dead—for us. Jesus.

> The Word became flesh and lived for a
> while among us. We have seen his glory, the
> glory of the one and only Son, who came
> from the Father, full of grace and truth.
> John 1:14 NIV

We could not climb to heaven. We could not
lift ourselves by our own bootstraps. We could
not progress to the state of bliss. We could only
receive our just wages of death. For anything to
accrue to our benefit, God had to do it.

God had to become flesh like us.

God had to let his Son die so we could see his
face.

God had to adopt us as sons and daughters.

God had to wash away our sins.

God had to change us to be like his Son.

God had to mercifully give us a ministry.

God has to make things grow.

God has to bring us unto himself.

Amazing Grace!

So we stand in holy awe, scarcely containing
our joy, looking into the face of Jesus and beholding God. Now we see more clearly that Jesus
is the Face of God—the invited-One in our blessing "Make his face shine upon you." More dis-
tinctly we hear Paul describe the depths of the
potential of this new revelation:

> My purpose is that they may be encour-
> aged in heart and united in love, so that
> they may have the full riches of complete
> understanding, in order that they may

know the mystery of God, namely, Christ,
in whom are hidden all the treasures of wisdom and knowledge. Colossians 2:2-3 NIV

There is more to his Face than we can behold
at once. We must take another look in the section of Meditations on the word "Face." There is
also more to his Name than we can behold at
once. We now make an astounding connection.

Connecting the Names

Now, we have attached "Face" and "Glory" to
Jesus. The Glory of Jesus revealed in the New
Testament is the same Glory of the Father as
revealed to Moses in the Old Testament. But
what of his Name?

When YHWH said to Moses, "This is the name
I am to be known by from generation to generation," where does this leave Jesus? Is Jesus an
aberration? Do we err by using his name? Is his
name temporary? Let us see.

To arrive at our destination, we need to walk
backward through the translation of the name
"Jesus." Jesus was not his actual name. That is
the way his name comes to us through the
Greek. Many, if not most, names will change
pronunciation when they are translated from
one language to another. For instance, Peter can
become Pedro, Paul can become Pablo, John can
become Ian or Sean, etc. This evidence prompts
an interesting chart:

Jesus = Joshua

Jesus' actual name was Joshua. Then, why haven't we been calling him that? I don't know, unless it was sometime, somewhere a conscious choice to call him the Greek Jesus so we could always tell him apart from all other Joshuas. But, we still have a problem here. You see, his name was not actually Joshua.

Joshua = Yahshua

Joshua is the way we pronounce his name when we anglicize the Hebrew pronunciation. His name was actually Yahshua. Now that we have reduced his name to its real root, we come to a glorious discovery that ties all eternity together. We know the meaning of the name Yahshua:

Yahshua = YHWH Saves

Incredible! YHWH has restored his name to us through Jesus. He no longer is unknown. Now we see his Face and know his Name. Now we see his Glory and know the meaning of his Name. Having this revelation answers several interesting theological problems in the New Testament which we explore in Part Five. Before we look at them, we must examine some of the ample proof that the name chart above is accurate.

> Jesus said unto them, Verily, verily, I
> say unto you, Before Abraham was, I am.
> John 8:58

What an audacious statement! To say he was the I AM could get him killed. The Jews knew immediately what he was claiming. There was no confusion in their minds. There was no hesitation in their reaction:

> Then took they up stones to cast at him:
> but Jesus hid himself, and went out of the
> temple, going through the midst of them,
> and so passed by. John 8:59

Had Jesus not been making a claim for himself in relationship to YHWH, the Jews would not have been so disturbed; they would only have considered Jesus disturbed. But the claims of Jesus were direct in meaning and, to the Jews, outrageous. It is difficult to be more direct in statement and the response more intense than in the following passage:

> I and my Father are one.
> Then the Jews took up stones again to
> stone him.
> Jesus answered them, Many good
> works have I shewed you from my Father;
> for which of those works do ye stone me?
> The Jews answered him, saying, For a
> good work we stone thee not; but for blas-
> phemy; and because that thou, being a
> man, makest thyself God.
> Jesus answered them, Is it not written
> in your law, I said, Ye are gods? If he called

them gods, unto whom the word of God came, and the scripture cannot be broken; Say ye of him, whom the Father hath sanctified, and sent into the world, Thou blasphemest; because I said, I am the Son of God? If I do not the works of my Father, believe me not. But if I do, though ye believe not me, believe the works: that ye may know, and believe, that the Father is in me, and I in him.

Therefore they sought again to take him: but he escaped out of their hand,.....
John 10:30-39

No misunderstanding exists in the passage we just read. Unbelief exists, but no misunderstanding. No question remained as to what Jesus had claimed for himself. Again, in their minds, he deserved death. "Who does he think he is? Claiming to be YHWH. Stone him!"

Evidence abounds that Jesus walked in the Name of YHWH—and in his power and nature—more than I can relate in this discussion, but we must examine the obvious. The strongest evidence comes to us during Passion Week—the final week before the crucifixion. Two remarkable statements occurred on that day we call "Palm Sunday" as Jesus made his entry into the City of Jerusalem in John 12:12,13.

On the next day much people that were come to the feast, when they heard that Jesus was coming to Jerusalem, took branches of palm trees, and went forth to meet him, and cried,

Hosanna:
Blessed is the King of Israel that cometh
in the name of the Lord.

"Hosanna." An old Hebrew expression used in praise. Its casual meaning is "save," or "save now" but its literal meaning includes the Name, YHWH. Thus, when the crowd waved and placed the palm branches and shouted to Jesus, they were shouting "YHWH save!"

This worship understanding of him could not be much clearer. The joyous irony of the moment which they may not have even understood was that they were making their praise request to the one whose name meant "YHWH saves!" So as they shouted the pleas of mankind, the answer was riding on the donkey. With a spiritual ear they would have heard:

"Hosanna!"
"Yahshua!"
"Hosanna!" (The plea)
"Yahshua!" (The response)

"YHWH save!"
"YHWH saves!"
"YHWH save!" (The plea)
"YHWH saves!" (The response)

The plea and the answer had met on this Jerusalem road. The people with palms, the King on a donkey. How unlikely a human drama. How burned with jealousy any other "prospective messiah" would have been at this moment. How like the way God works. How direct the use of the Name. Indeed, that is the other revelation of their praise—the Name.

> Blessed is the King of Israel that cometh in the name of the Lord. John 12:13

The people knew whose Name was on the banner of the donkey rider—the Name of the Lord. By revelation now and by experience earlier, they had discovered that the one they now honored had consistently honored and lived the Name of the Father. They had watched him be:

Compassionate
Gracious
Slow to anger
Abounding in love
Abounding in faithfulness
Maintaining love to thousands
Forgiving wickedness
Forgiving rebellion
Forgiving sin

He had come in the Father's Name and in his Nature. The YHWH of eternity was riding by on a donkey. They knew it. The children, citizens of the kingdom of Heaven, knew it. (Matthew 21:15,16) Heaven and earth had met. Righteousness and peace had kissed each other.

But the most direct, even blatant, claim was to come just a few days later in a prayer:

"I have manifested thy name unto the men which thou gavest me out of the world: thine they were, and thou gavest them me; and they have kept thy word." John 17:6

"All I have is yours, and all you have is mine. And glory has come to me through them. I will remain in the world no longer, but they are still in the world, and I am coming to you. Holy Father, protect them by the power of your name—the name you gave me— so that they may be one as we are one. While I was with them, I protected them and kept them safe by that name you gave me." 10-12 NIV

Jesus declares that the name of the Father was the name given to himself. What other proof do we need? The revelation is complete; the Name is restored; God, Emmanuel, is with us. Joy to the world, the Lord is come!

Which Name Should I Use?

We return to an earlier discussion about the true pronunciation of the name of God. Having come to some probable conclusions about the Father, we must consider how that affects our look at Jesus. The name "Jesus" appears to be a rather strained attempt to bring Yahshua into Greek. The name "Jesus" is accepted because of common usage, not because of accuracy.

If we demand absolute accuracy of our translations, then we must print YHWH rather than LORD and Yahshua rather than Jesus. (Orthodox Jews would not pronounce YHWH and would likely write Yahshua as Y'shua or Yeshua.) Therefore, if you were a literalist on the names, you would read YHWH for the Father and say Yahshua for Jesus.

However, please let me repeat an earlier statement. The real understanding (I hope I have made this clear) is that God's nature is attached firmly to his name. *If we hit his name and miss his nature, we have violated him regardless of how smug we may feel about our accuracy.* I repeat again another earlier statement: I am comfortable in personal prayer and communication with God using the names Yahweh and Yahshua. In communication with other people, I freely use the common terms "Lord" and "Jesus" for the sake of understanding. We are free to use the actual names, but I don't think God intended for divisions to come over that subject.

One final note (again, a repeat), YHWH gave us that Name to remember him; Yahshua gave us bread and wine to remember him. Let us not *forget.* That is the point.

THE FATHER STYLE

Part Five

THE FRUIT

In the Name of Jesus

When I was a child, I concluded that the words "in the name of Jesus" were magic words—magic words that you used at the end of every prayer to make it valid. I thought it didn't matter what you prayed as long as you said, "in the name of Jesus." And, if you forgot to say those magic words at the end of the prayer, you destroyed the whole prayer. It was not official until you used the magic words.

I understand how anyone could come to that conclusion. Jesus himself almost empowers that "magic" statement with these statements:

> And whatsoever ye shall ask in my name, that will I do, that the Father may be glorified in the Son. If ye shall ask any thing in my name, I will do it. John 14:13,14
>
> Ye have not chosen me, but I have chosen you, and ordained you, that ye should go and bring forth fruit, and that your fruit should remain: that whatsoever ye shall ask of the Father in my name, he may give it you. 15:16
>
> And in that day ye shall ask me nothing. Verily, verily, I say unto you, Whatsoever ye shall ask the Father in my name, he will give it you. Hitherto have ye asked nothing in my name: ask, and ye shall receive, that your joy may be full. 16:23-24

This sort of authoritative statement, "in my name," launches whole denominations who feel they have grasped a certain truth ignored by others. But I have discovered something about this set of words that resolves many, if not all, of the swirling controversies about asking "in the name of Jesus."

First, I believe that Jesus never meant for his name to be used in some "magic word" incantation. Sure indication of that comes from his strong statements in Matthew (My emphasis):

> Many will say to me in that day, Lord, Lord, have we not prophesied *in thy name?* and *in thy name* have cast out devils? and *in thy name* done many wonderful works? And then will I profess unto them, I never knew you: depart from me, ye that work iniquity. Matthew 7:22-23

Obviously, the use of his name is effectual, but, in some cases, counterproductive according to these statements of Jesus. Castaways, all of them: though they used his name they didn't use his nature. This is strong evidence that his name is more than simply the correct order of certain letters and words.

Frankly, these verses perplex me. My logic says that these are great things done for the right reason using the right name. Obviously, Jesus knows more about our hearts than we do. This statement destroys all boasting as Jesus informs the subjects who misuse his name that he would say he never knew them.

Is it possible to use his name effectively without being followers ourselves? Apparently so. One of the Ten Commandments tells us not to misuse his name. It is grating to see individuals of questionable ethics using the name of Jesus. I want to arise and shout "Not fair!" I want to lead an exposé move. But God has a better way. He says, "Leave it to me. I want to see good things done—even by bad people. I will handle the bad people in my own time."

In Philippians 1, Paul the Apostle did not complain that bad people were preaching the Good News in a bad way. He was just glad that Jesus was being preached. I can see I have a long way to go before I can react that way.

Another dramatic lesson comes to us from Acts:

> Some Jews who went around driving out evil spirits tried to invoke the name of the Lord Jesus over those who were demon-possessed. They would say, "In the name of Jesus, whom Paul preaches, I command you to come out." Seven sons of Sceva, a Jewish chief priest, were doing this. The evil spirit answered them, "Jesus I know and Paul I know about, but who are you?" Then the man who had the evil spirit jumped on them and overpowered them all. He gave them such a beating that they ran out of the house naked and bleeding. 19:13-16 NIV

I chuckle every time I read this passage. Not only did the demons *not* come out, the demon-empowered man almost beat these seven sons to death. They ran away screaming and naked.

The sons of Sceva used the right words—even making sure the evil spirits understood just which Jesus they were talking about, "the one whom Paul preaches," but that was still not a proper use of his name. The results in this case as well as the passage in Matthew 7 were very embarrassing to the central figures. Merely using the set of words, "in the name of Jesus," though sometimes effective, is not asking "in his name."

These seven sons felt that they had special psychic powers because of their birth situation. In this one moment Jesus proved the bankruptcy of the whole occult scene. Whatever you call yourself—new wave, red wave or permanent wave—don't try to cast out any demons unless you are a true follower of Jesus. The truth is: you can't cast Satan out by using Satan. So, don't try to use the name of Jesus unless you use it in his nature.

In My Name Means In My Nature

Insight into this truth—his "name" means his "nature"—comes simply by understanding the use of one's "name" in the same way that the people of the day of Jesus would use it. To do something "in the name" of a person was to do it the way they would do it. For instance, suppose I were stealing a piece of equipment and you see me. The conversation could go like this:

"What are you doing?"

"I'm taking this piece of equipment."

"Why?"

"Because Roger told me to."

"Oh no! Roger would never tell you to do that."

In other words, I could not steal something in the name of an honest man. I could not lie in the name of a truthful man. If I do something in someone's name, I must also do it in accordance with the nature of that person, else it is not in his name.

Thus, in order to *ask*, "in the name of Jesus," I must ask for something in keeping with his nature or else it is not in his name. In order for me to *do* something "in the name of Jesus," it must be something that he would do himself or that fits in his nature. Consequently, any prayer of mine that would have God's ear, must be:

Compassionate
Gracious
Slow to anger
Abounding in love
Abounding in faithfulness
Maintaining love to thousands
Forgiving wickedness
Forgiving rebellion
Forgiving sin

Anything I do that would please the Father must also fit that pattern. Pleasantly, another verse from John becomes intensely logical:

> If ye abide in me, and my words abide in you, ye shall ask what ye will, and it shall be done unto you. John 15:7

The words of Jesus in us and our intimacy with him can only produce his nature in us. Thus, when we ask, we can only think to ask something that would fit within his nature which would then guarantee our answers. God is interested only in prayers that fit in with his nature and grand scheme. We can only pray those prayers when we are steeped in the character of our God, otherwise we fall prey to our greedy humanity and the wrong things happen. James talks about it:

> You want something but don't get it. You kill and covet, but you cannot have what you want. You quarrel and fight. You do not have, because you do not ask God. When you ask, you do not receive, because you ask with wrong motives, that you may spend what you get on your pleasures. James 4:2,3 NIV

God has no stake in selfish praying no matter what set of words we use. We can be flowery and eloquent. We can even pray in unity. We can pray in great sincerity. We can invoke "the name of Jesus." But, unless the prayer matches the unselfish, loving nature of Jesus, the Father is not compelled to answer as we wish. John drives another nail in this board in his first epistle:

> And this is the confidence that we have in him, that, if we ask anything according to his will, he heareth us: And if we know that he hear us, whatsoever we ask, we know that we have the petitions that we desired of him. 1 John 5:14,15

So, praying in the name of Jesus also means praying in accordance with his will. Since Jesus "delighted" in doing the Father's will and even said his "meat" was to do the will of the Father, it is logical that his nature matched the will of the Father as did his name.

This understanding now becomes a powerful ally of ours. If we long to have power in prayer, then pray in his name, i.e., in accordance with his nature. Pray for the things for which Jesus would pray. Intercessory prayer takes on a whole new meaning in our hearts. Selfish praying becomes poison. Now, we can even understand how "seeking first his kingdom" can produce such promised results. (Matthew 6:33)

Foundations are now in place for us to explore old areas of Scripture and to see new, now obvious, answers to old problems. Since we have been talking about using his name, prayer is a good place to begin.

The Lord's Prayer

> After this manner therefore pray ye:
> Our Father which art in heaven, Hallowed
> be thy name. Thy kingdom come. Thy will
> be done in earth, as it is in heaven. Give us
> this day our daily bread. And forgive us our
> debts, as we forgive our debtors. And lead
> us not into temptation, but deliver us from
> evil: For thine is the kingdom, and the
> power, and the glory, for ever. Amen.
> Matthew 6:9-13

HALLOWED BE THY NAME

Hasn't everything been said about the Lord's Prayer? No. When you see the traits in the name of the Father, this prayer takes on a whole new understanding. If you look at this prayer through the lens of Exodus 34, certain words immediately stand out—"name," "will," "today," "forgive," "glory." New power comes to our praying when we express to the Father the qualities he outlined in the revelation of his name. Praise overflows as we hallow his name—compassion, grace, longsuffering, love, faithfulness, forgiveness.

When we see the meaning of his name, we have all the more reason to honor him. Hallowing his name is not merely being careful to avoid all use of his name as a swear word. Hallowing his name is not carefully sewing his name to our casual clothing or a banner. Hallowing his name is not putting his name over our church door. To hallow (honor) his name is to recognize the nature represented and to ascribe that nature to God in praise.

To hallow his name properly will take more time than we usually spend on the Lord's Prayer, but ascribing that greatness to him fulfills the pattern Jesus has taught us. Part of any such honor could be called celebration. We have holidays to celebrate persons or events of history. Such celebration is our means of honoring or hallowing. Other events in our spiritual walk become means of honoring, hallowing or celebrating, once we see the meaning of his name.

Jesus told us to partake of the bread and wine to remember (celebrate, honor, hallow) him. So sadly ritualized, this important event, Communion, is the authorized fireworks of our freedom. What shall we remember? "We will remember the Name of the Lord our God." (Psalms 20:7) Does that mean knowing how his name sounds? Not necessarily. Remembering means knowing what his name means. That is what we celebrate. So the Eucharist, Communion, the Lord's Supper becomes part of the prayer of our life as we hallow his name.

Imagine the new adventures in worship as we meditate on and say to God the meaning of his name to us. If we spoke to the Lord of our joy and appreciation for each facet of the compassion list from Exodus 34 and the servant list from the life of Jesus, prayer would never again decline into mere ritualism.

THY KINGDOM COME

This is a very personal request: "Father, I want you to dominate me—be king in my life." Certainly, it is a reasonable request once we have seen the nature of the Father. We can pick our kingdoms. Paul tells us that we are slaves to whomever we choose to yield ourselves—sin or righteousness. No one in his right mind would ever want to be yielded to Satan, so Satan must deceive about his kingship and portray it as glamorous, and lie about the kingdom of God and portray it as prudish and boring.

What a settling way to start a day in prayer: "God, dominate me. Rule in my life. Let my actions portray that you are in control of me."

THY WILL BE DONE

Now that we know the traits of his will, we can pray more profitably. We affirmed his nature at the beginning of the prayer, established his dominance in our second statement and now turn our thoughts toward affecting our world. Praying in God's will, 1 John 5:14,15 tells us, guarantees success in prayer. The progression of the Lord's prayer guarantees that we will pray in his will. Since, by his nature, we know what God desires for us and we know how he is toward us, prayer for others and for the fulfillment of his kingdom becomes more focused. We can truly intercede. We can free the hand of God to move our world.

GIVE US THIS DAY OUR DAILY BREAD

I know God ignores a selfish prayer, but I still find my corrupt heart longing for tomorrow's bread. I can make a good argument to the Lord about how effective I can be for him if he would supply me with enough advance funds. It is a little frightening to pray for "today's bread." That means I must pray again tomorrow and believe again for tomorrow. My greedy heart is willing to be corrupted by a little bit of riches so that I can see my warehouse full of loaves. I can even make a good argument about how God won't have to be bothered with me every day if he would only advance me about ten year's worth of bread.

Having prayed the first part of the prayer, light falls on my darker recesses and brings my greed under his control. "Today's bread" is not only a corrective prayer for my greed, but one that fits his will enough to be answered. In all things, including my desire for prosperity, the nature of my Lord takes precedent.

FORGIVE

Just the word seems sufficient, now. We know that forgiveness is a major part of the nature of God. It is an act of faith to ask for God's forgiveness, an act of growth and maturity to ask to be made like him in forgiving. The focus of the words points my thoughts outside myself for the benefit of others. Sounds like something God would do.

THINE IS...THE GLORY

No person or thing in this life can achieve the glory that left the Apostles speechless on the Mount of Transfiguration and the shepherds awestruck outside Bethlehem. Any pretender to the throne of our lives merely camouflages evil with fraudulent vapor. God will not share his Glory. Not one thing short of God himself wraps us in the grace and forgiveness or the love and the patience that the Creator has designed for us. Our spouses were not created to fill that need. If we expect them to provide what God's glory has reserved for itself, we equate our spouses with God and place undue pressure on them. Our jobs do no better at meeting the basic needs of our lives. God will not share his glory. Money, pleasure—any of the world's attempts to find meaning in life—are destined to fail. God will not share his glory. Only *he* is the author of grace. Our denominations and other Christian organizations become attempts to capture, store and preserve some facsimile of God's Glory. We desperately hope that grace will flow to us through that heritage. If Glory could be so en- trapped, then our organizations would not shrivel and die as history tells us they all do. Glory is privately distributed by the great "Thou" of eternity. Thine is the glory forever and ever. Amen.

Now that we have refreshed our view of prayer in the shadow of his Name and Glory, that same shadow relieves another festering sore around the subject of baptism.

Baptism

Baptism split the church early in its history. That historical tendency survives to this day. If you want to start an argument quickly among Christians, simply try to decide when and how someone is to be baptized, whose hands and whose water and how much is to be used. One particularly intense controversy comes out of Acts 2:38:

> Then Peter said unto them, Repent, and be baptized every one of you in the name of Jesus Christ for the remission of sins, and ye shall receive the gift of the Holy Ghost.

Some interpret this passage to be the overriding definition for the baptismal formula. Many of those who hold to this position feel that Jesus' injunction to baptize "in the name of the Father and of the Son and of the Holy Spirit" (Matthew 28:19) was to say that the "name" of the Father, Son and Spirit was "Jesus." Although I disagree with this premise, that is not the point I wish to confront. The real issue has to do, once again, with the nature of God. Since the nature of YHWH and Yahshua and the Holy Spirit are the same, to baptize someone in their name(s) or to simply say "in the name of Jesus" is to baptize the person into the compassion, grace,...forgiveness, etc., of God.

Once this concept is understood, no true problem remains. On the other hand, if one is baptized as a hostile and divisive act and not into compassion, grace..., then he is not baptized into God regardless of which "name" is used. Division comes when emphasis is put upon the set of letters used to designate a name and not on the nature that the name represents.

Once we see the power of his nature in restoring the simplicity of baptism, it is obvious that the name heals the damage of our divisive actions and theologies once we understand the meaning of the name. Understanding the meaning frees us to move ahead and see how the Name can be used to heal another very serious rift that has existed for generations—our divisions, denominations, exclusions.

Gatherings

Have you ever entered a church building that had God's name over the door, but, once inside, you could not detect the presence of God? I think you know what I mean. Then in the midst of the "God-absent" gathering, you remembered these words of Jesus:

> For where two or three are gathered together in my name, there am I in the midst of them. Matthew 18:20

You realize that there must be some paradox here or else the presence of the Lord is so well hidden and powerless as to be undetectable in some gatherings. How does our premise of the name/nature of Jesus answer this dichotomy? Very easily. Whether we use his name to identify our gatherings ultimately means very little. The real question is whether we are gathered around compassion, grace...forgiveness...etc. If we are not gathered around the nature of our Lord, then we are not gathered in his name regardless of the words over the doors of our buildings.

If we are gathered around his nature, there will be evidence of his presence whether we even have a name over the door or not. Any argument over the *name* of a church or even *The* Church is totally spurious and ignorant. The real question is not the name over the door, but what the nature is inside.

At last we have come to a point of closure. With the Apostles, we have heard the answer to the great question, "Show us the Father." We know what the Father is like. He is like Jesus. We know what Jesus is like. He is like the Father. Full of Grace and Truth. It is enough.

Some Final Observations

Except for the meditations in the remaining chapter of this book, we have come to the end of our journey through the revelations of the nature of the Father and the Son. We can safely reach certain conclusions:

1. God is truly good beyond our deepest understanding.
2. The Law has been fulfilled, but his mercy continues to be renewed every day.
3. Since this is true, if we feel separated from God, our feelings are lying to us. The God of compassion moves toward us in our inadequacies. Let us open our hearts to him.

The theme of the first four parts of this book has been very simple. That theme is: God is known best by his own descriptions of himself. The descriptions that best describe him are the defining of his name to Moses in Exodus 34 and the teaching of Jesus about himself when he taught on "The Greatest in the Kingdom."

Sub-themes are that the Name of the Lord and his Glory are identical in definition and substance and that Jesus, who carries God's Name and expresses his Glory, is the Face of God. With this understanding, you will never hear the words "Name," "Face," or "Glory" without thinking new thoughts about God. It is my hope that you will bask in the reality of his grace. Blessed be the Name of the Lord.

To secure our understanding of his nature and open windows for fresh knowledge of his Name, Glory and Face, let us move to Part Six and ponder the revelations God has made through these words.

THE FATHER STYLE

Part Six

MEDITATIONS

The Name

The doors opened by our new understanding of Name, Face and Glory invite us to walk new and scenic spiritual trails. To assist you in that walk, I have chosen some references to those word concepts from the scripture and presented them in this chapter under their three headings as meditations or devotional moments. Hopefully, they will be helpers of your joy.

Power Show

> But I have raised you [Pharaoh] up for this very purpose, that I might show you my power and that my name might be proclaimed in all the earth. Exodus 9:16 NIV

The great Pharaohs did everything they could to establish themselves. Their pyramid tombs still survive and are the object of much tourist interest. Their power seemed unstoppable. But the Pharaohs didn't count on a scruffy little band of slaves who had an unusually vigorous God. Who did these Israelites think they were, anyway, to challenge the great one with some stuttering sheepherder who had to speak through his brother?

Pharaoh thought himself to be a god, but little did he know that he was only a pawn in the plans of the great YHWH, the Name. Had he known what he, Pharaoh, was truly about—to glorify the great YHWH, he then could have been proud. Actually, when we think about it, we are all created for his pleasure and his glory. For all of us, our reason for being is to proclaim his Name in all the earth.

No "Cussing"

> Thou shalt not take the name of the LORD thy God in vain; for the LORD will not hold him guiltless that taketh his name in vain. Exodus 20:7

"Don't cuss," is what I always heard in relationship to this verse, "because that's taking the Lord's Name in vain." True, it means that, because cursing is inappropriate to the Name of the Lord, but obviously this means more than "cussing." When God says not to misuse his Name, he is talking about any use that does not fit with his compassionate, gracious, forgiving nature. If we take on his Name or call on his Name or proclaim his Name for selfish purposes, we have misused it. How often has his Name been used to justify social evil or greedy fundraising or selfish ambition! To use God's Name is to accept his demands. He writes a very rigid contract about his Name. If we choose to call an institution "Christian," whether it is a college, church or parachurch organization (or our nation, if we choose to call it "Christian"), and by its actions it violates in any way the nature of our YHWH, then that institution has drunk the poison of its death. Politicians who choose to identify themselves with Christians and try to lay claim to Christian principles to garner votes have tread on ground more dangerous than they know. Any army that fights under the banner of God had best learn the use of *non-carnal* weapons. God's Name is to be honored not misused. Any misuse of his Name should cause us to tremble until it is rectified.

Leave Us Alone

> When the people saw the thunder and lightning and heard the trumpet and saw the mountain in smoke, they trembled with fear. They stayed at a distance and said to Moses, "Speak to us yourself and we will listen. But do not have God speak to us or we will die." Moses said to the people, "Do not be afraid. God has come to test you, so that the fear of God will be with you to keep you from sinning." The people remained at a distance, while Moses approached the thick darkness where God was. Then the LORD said to Moses, "Tell the Israelites this: 'You have seen for yourselves that I have spoken to you from heaven:...'"
> Exodus 20:18-22 NIV

A terrible decision this is, "Do not have God speak to us." At this moment they opted to remove themselves from intimacy with God. They would, from this day forward, truly know him only through the Law. Moses, on the other hand, would achieve a closeness that would include seeing the back parts of God and beholding his Glory, but the Israelites would only hear about it second-hand.

In Deuteronomy 10, when Moses was giving final reminders about their entry into the Promised Land, he told the story about receiving the second set of the Ten Commandments but omitted the details about the revelation of the Nature of the Father. Why? Most likely because the Israelites had chosen silence and distance from God. They did not have to decide for silence and distance, nor do we. God does not operate by remote control. His nature is understood only by those who are near and want to hear.

If you have any former contracts with God that remove you from intimacy, erase them all now and draw near to where the Glory is.

Record Keeper

> ...in all places where I record my name
> I will come unto thee, and I will bless thee.
> Exodus 20:24

What else do we need to affirm the sovereignty of God? God even controls his own honor. If we think we are in charge of such honor or are the source of such honor, surprise! God does not leave it up to the whims of human emotion; he will cause the honor.

God could have said, "Since you don't honor me, I will..." or "Since I can trust you to honor me, I will..." He could have been vindictive and sought vengeance because of our lack of honor, but his overwhelming grace wins again; God shows his true colors. He sets up the party in his own honor, invites us to attend and then blesses us because he was honored. This is too good. Pack-of-losers that we are, we win again!

Pay Attention

> Pay attention to him [my Angel] and listen to him...since my Name is in him.
> Exodus 23:21 NIV

How do we decide who the authority is? To whom do we listen? Find out who has the Name of God in him and he is worth hearing. Find out who walks in grace and forgiveness and you have just discerned who knows God.

Strong evidence exists that this "Angel" may well have been Jesus himself—good reason to listen. Later, the Father would say of Jesus, "This is my son whom I dearly love. Listen to him!" If I want to hear truth and gain knowledge and probe wisdom, I know where to go—to the one who has the Name in him, Jesus.

How to Bless

> And the LORD spake unto Moses, say-
> ing, Speak unto Aaron and unto his sons,
> saying, On this wise ye shall bless the chil-
> dren of Israel, saying unto them, The LORD
> bless thee, and keep thee: The LORD make
> his face shine upon thee, and be gracious
> unto thee: The LORD lift up his counte-
> nance upon thee, and give thee peace. And
> they shall put my name upon the children
> of Israel; and I will bless them.
> Numbers 6:22-27

This familiar passage has been memorized, recited and sung to our great benefit for many years. God instructs the sons of Aaron to bless the people. This means that people would learn to expect blessing from anyone who represented God. Something has changed, hasn't it? Now, we don't always expect blessing when we en-counter a "man of God." Indeed, I sometimes will turn the sound off on a television preacher to see if I can discern from his face and motions what is being said. Usually I see expressions of anger while supposedly declaring God's love. It is rare to see blessing communicated. But God appointed the priests for blessing.

The real theme of this meditation comes from the last verse: God has given us the power to place His Name on people by blessing them. God has given each of us a heavenly stamp-pad with his Name and we can, by blessing each other, stamp his Name on people. What an incredible opportunity! "The Lord bless you..." Stamp, stamp! "The Lord bless you..." Stamp, stamp!

Levi Genes

> At that time the LORD separated the tribe of Levi, to bear the ark of the covenant of the LORD, to stand before the LORD to minister unto him, and to bless in his name, unto this day. Deuteronomy 10:8

The Levites had three jobs that would be the envy of anyone: First, they carried the "mercy seat," the Ark of the Covenant. Second, they worshiped (ministered to) the Lord. Third, they blessed the people.

I have decided that I want to be a carrier of his mercy. In a sense, we each carry a pot in our arms that contains what we are. When people bump our elbows (and they will!), whatever is in that pot spills on them. If the pot is filled with vinegar, vinegar spills. If it's honey, honey spills. When people bump me (and they will!), I want to spill mercy on them. I want to fulfill my created purpose—to glorify God and to bless people in his Name.

To carry the Mercy Seat around was to carry hope around. That Ark was a traveling promise! Even its enemies and captors recognized its power and representation. Anyone privileged to see it must have exploded in worship. To worship the Lord is to achieve our highest. Worship is the natural response to the presence of his highest in the Mercy Seat. Blessing the people, the one activity oriented toward mankind, was to be done "in his Name." The people were to know that this blessing was "compliments" of the creator and was typical of his nature.

Finally, such blessing was not destined to cease. We are still to bless the people in his Name. True, the Melchizedek priesthood has superseded the "birth-order" priesthood of the Levites with a rebirth-order, but the main change is that the priesthood is now available for all and the blessing is greater. We are still commanded to carry his grace, to worship and to bless. Amen.

A Song to the Rock

> I will proclaim the name of the LORD. Oh, praise the greatness of our God! He is the Rock, his works are perfect, and all his ways are just. A faithful God who does no wrong, upright and just is he. Deuteronomy 32:3,4 NIV

This verse is from the Song of Moses. Great songs come from our experiences. Just as God had preached his Name to Moses, Moses would now preach God's Name to the world. Moses would not forget the Rock that protected him on that mountain nor the message that surrounded that Name—greatness, perfection, justice, faithfulness, righteousness, uprightness.

The more I experience God in his truth, the more my heart sings of his nature. It seems that when revival comes, a fresh wave of vibrant creativity accompanies it: new songs flow from the pens of inspired people; new methods reach into untouched hearts; new forms of unity arise. I want to proclaim his Name and listen to the vibrations of my soul.

A Happy God

> For the sake of his great name the LORD will not reject his people, because the LORD was pleased to make you his own.
> 1 Samuel 12:22 NIV

The people had rejected God's rule and wanted a king. Their desire had been granted and Samuel was giving final instructions to this rebellious people with their rebellious king. We cannot fail to see the working of the nature of God in this passage: It was not the worthiness of the people that caused God to favor them, not at all! Only God's own graceful nature caused him not to reject the people. God is consistent. His pleasure is in his own work. He receives us—his workmanship—with pleasure. Blessed be the Name of the Lord!

Look This Way

> May your eyes be open toward this temple night and day, this place of which you said, "My Name shall be there," so that you will hear the prayer your servant prays toward this place. 1 Kings 8:29 NIV

If you want to know a man's heart, listen to him pray. Here, the temple is being dedicated and this passage comes from the great prayer of Solomon. Solomon understands the presence of "The Name." Because his Name, YHWH, was there, this temple was to be the center of compassion, grace, longsuffering, love, faithfulness and forgiveness. Unfortunately, it became the center of the Law and man lost his understanding of God as he focused his attention on himself and his own righteousness.

The New Covenant brought to us by Jesus, has given us a different understanding about where God dwells and consequently where his Name and compassion dwell. We know that God does not dwell in a temple made by hands. We know that he now dwells with man—we have become his temple.

Ah, now it is time for a new prayer of dedication—a prayer for the new temple, *ourselves*. When we do pray the prayer that the location of his compassion be in us, we can expect his glory to overwhelm this new temple!

Overdue Bill

Give unto the LORD, ye kindreds of the people, give unto the LORD glory and strength. Give unto the LORD the glory due unto his name: bring an offering, and come before him: worship the LORD in the beauty of holiness. 1 Chronicles 16:28,29

Now, we listen to a song of David. The occasion? The "Mercy Seat," the Ark of the Covenant has been retrieved and David bursts into song and dance. Whenever the Mercy Seat is present, our souls dance, our spirits sing. The Ark is forever home now in the temple of our hearts. Now the Mercy Seat is ever present in Jesus. Dance, my soul, dance!

In the presence of his Mercy Seat, the glory of his compassionate, gracious and forgiving Name is worth our comment. It takes strength to be compassionate. God has that strength.

Name Calling

If my people, which are called by my name, shall humble themselves, and pray, and seek my face, and turn from their wicked ways; then will I hear from heaven, and will forgive their sin, and will heal their land. 2 Chronicles 7:14

For now have I chosen and sanctified this house, that my name may be there for ever: and mine eyes and mine heart shall be there perpetually. 16

Solomon's prayer recorded in 1 Kings 8 was a noble prayer that reached the height of devotion. It was magnificent. However, Solomon wanted to provide for all expected situations. What if, rather than being humble and righteous, the people became arrogant and wicked? What if these people on whom God had placed his Name, turned away? Can they come back? Will God receive them? That very Name, it seems, would urge us to repentance, humility and prayer.

The God who is near and compassionate promises that his eyes will be open and his ear attentive. What else could we ask. Like Moses, let us fall on our faces before his Face (Jesus) so that our prayers may be unhindered.

The Bigger Chariot

> Some trust in chariots, and some in horses: but we will remember the name of the LORD our God. Psalm 20:7

Just how much money does the world spend on defense? What redirection of prosperity would occur if we all beat our swords into plowshares, converted our guns into farming implements? Chariots and horses are the works of man—his desperate attempt to achieve security. Funny thing about security—it is never quite achieved, so we get more horses and build bigger chariots. Then we discover that personal security is not that simple. We must now build bigger houses, barns and bank accounts and buy more guns. These are the chariots of our lives.

There are spiritual chariots, also. We can lean on our ability to live within the rules or the correctness of our theology or the age and stability of our denomination. They are chariots, all. Or...

We can trust in his Name—the compassionate, gracious, forgiving one. Then the swords of our own hearts can be beaten into useful instruments of production. When all else fails, and you can be sure it will, remember the Name. Better yet, don't wait for failure. Remember his Name now.

Endurance

> His name shall endure for ever: his name shall be continued as long as the sun: and men shall be blessed in him: all nations shall call him blessed. Blessed be the LORD God, the God of Israel, who only doeth wondrous things. And blessed be his glorious name for ever: and let the whole earth be filled with his glory; Amen, and Amen.
> Psalm 72:17-19

Environmental concerns have shown us that some things, such as toxic wastes, last longer than we want; and some things, such as our fuel supply and our automobiles, do not last as long as we wish.

If you were to sit down and list those things you would want to have endure for a lifetime and then be passed along to your heirs, you would likely come up with the statement in the scripture above. If his Name endures forever, your children are well cared for. If all nations are blessed through him, your children will live in peace. If the only marvelous deeds are done by God, your children will not be deceived by life nor destroyed by wastes. If the earth is filled with his glory—his compassion, grace and forgiveness—your children will lack nothing that matters in life. Indeed, may his Name last as long as the sun. No, even longer—forever!

Say "Thank You"

> Unto thee, O God, do we give thanks, unto thee do we give thanks: for that thy name is near thy wondrous works declare.
> Psalm 75:1

Throughout history, mankind has sought ways to appease false dieties whom they considered to be capricious and vicious or to contact false dieties whom they considered to be distant. Man's ignorance and disobedience hid the truth—all along, the Lord is near. The coming of his Son speaks Emmanuel closeness to us. John the Beloved assures us that they did not only see and hear him, but they *touched* him. God is near and he wants us to know that.

There is nothing you can do to bring God closer to you. He is near. There is nothing you can do to drive him away. He is near. So, what can we do? We can walk in the nearness of his grace with thankful hearts and tell of his wonderful deeds.

...One Heart, Indivisible, with...

> Teach me your way, O LORD, and I will walk in your truth; give me an undivided heart, that I may fear your name. Psalm 86:11 NIV

When my heart is divided; when I haven't made up my mind, I am useless. When I "halt between two opinions," it truly brings me to a halt. If I am being chased and I can't decide where to run, I am caught. A divided heart eats up all our energy. "A house divided against itself cannot stand." A divided heart is a confused mind that does not know who to respect or accept as authority. "Blessed are the pure in heart for they will see God." Jesus, in the great Beatitudes, proposes the same solution. "Pure in heart" means an undivided heart—singleness of mind. Such an undivided heart sees God and properly respects (fears) his Name. Rather than "halt between two opinions," we advance with unified mind and heart. Ah, but again it is the gift of God that our heart be undivided. "Lord, teach and give. We receive."

Not Me

> Not unto us, O LORD, not unto us, but unto thy name give glory, for thy mercy, and for thy truth's sake. Psalm 115:1

> I am the LORD: that is my name: and my glory will I not give to another, neither my praise to graven images. Isaiah 42:8

If there is anything my flesh loves to do, it is to take the credit, to receive the glory. My flesh loves to think that its own skills are all that are needed to supply security or any other need. My flesh revels in praise, in introductions before crowds, or in articles in newspapers. My flesh thrills to be noticed as outstanding—beautiful or handsome or intelligent. My flesh hungers for the glory and when wisdom overtakes me and I finally try to starve the flesh, I find that it is a pesky critter that subsists on junk food.

We pursue salvation in the flesh. It is pursued through our spouses, jobs, money, friends, positions, honors, even through drugs, alcohol and sex. Surely, we think, if one doesn't satisfy, the other will, so we join the chase. "In pursuit of happiness" aptly describes us.

However, God refuses to let the flesh get away with such a lie. Glory is reserved for himself. Grace flows only from the heart of the Father. Don't seek it anywhere else. If any thought arises that you might save yourself, squash it! Hide the junk food from your flesh!

This Is the House

> Blessed be he that cometh in the name
> of the LORD: we have blessed you out of the
> house of the LORD. Psalm 118:26

What moves a crowd? A national anthem? A victory in the world games? A celebration of political triumph? All of the above. But, what could move a Jerusalem Passover crowd to begin to strip palm trees and run toward a city entrance? What could excite a heart enough to lay those palm branches in the path of a person riding a small donkey? What could cause them to throw their clothes in his path to make a carpet? What could cause them to earnestly shout "hosanna?" Could it be some Zealot would-be Messiah gathering an army to fight Rome? Unlikely. Those Zealots do not know the palm-fronds of peace. Is it an Olympic games winner? Unlikely. The crown of thorns, the medal given to the completer of this race, is going to be a bit uncomfortable. Is it a political celebration? Unlikely. No one wants the death-robes that will soon surround this "king." Then why run so hard to see this person? Something eternal must be happening. Someone must be coming in the Name of the Lord. Compassion, grace and forgiveness just mounted a donkey and entered town. Bring me a palm to wave. I want to shout "hosanna" to the right person!

Invincible Duo

> I will bow down toward your holy temple
> and will praise your name for your love and
> your faithfulness, for you have exalted
> above all things your name and your word.
> Psalm 138:2 NIV

Take a look around you. All you see is going to pass away. Imagine it melting; eventually it will. Touch the material things that are important to you. Imagine them turning to dust. They will. Look at the Word of God. See it living forever. It will. Breathe the Name of God. See its mercy enduring forever. It will. When all else manifests its smallness, the Name and the Word stand high. Let us proclaim his Name and hide his Word in our hearts.

Safe Tower

> The name of the LORD is a strong tower;
> the righteous run to it and are safe.
> Proverbs 18:10 NIV

Had I been writing the Bible from some of my erroneous understandings, I would have written, "The Name of the Lord is a strong terror; the sinner runs from it to find safety." Fortunately, God had a better idea. Once we understand the meaning of his Name, to run away in terror is absurd. Why would we run from compassion and mercy? Why would we ever want to escape forgiveness?

The righteous man is unearthly wise. He is not righteous because he is so much better than others or so much smarter or so much more heavenly. He is righteous because he knows where to run. The Name of the Lord is a tower, not for the cowardly but for the wise. The wise man knows his need and where his only hope lies. In that strong tower—his Name—nothing can touch you. Nothing!

Catch That Aroma

> Pleasing is the fragrance of your perfumes; your name is like perfume poured out. No wonder the maidens love you!
> Song of Solomon 1:3 NIV

Perfumes have always been expensive and have driven trading ships for centuries to exotic ports. Originally, perfumes were not applied to provide an odor, they were applied to cover other odors. Now, they are also designed to attract. Whatever you need a perfume to do, God provides the best—his Name. Our imperfections, our dirt, our malodorous sins cry desperately for something to cover them. God provides.

We know ourselves to be terribly unattractive, our spirits mangled by every conceivable perversion. Can anything ever give us beauty again? Ah, yes. There is a heavenly cosmetic. "No wonder the maidens love you."

Broad Shouldered Baby

> For unto us a child is born, unto us a
> son is given: and the government shall be
> upon his shoulder: and his name shall be
> called Wonderful, Counselor, The mighty
> God, The everlasting Father, The Prince of
> Peace. Isaiah 9:6

Handel's "Messiah" marches through my
heart as I read the scripture above. My spirit is
carried away. My heart yearns for the government to be on the shoulders of the man of grace,
compassion and forgiveness. Having a "wonderful lawyer" is almost beyond imagination. God,
mighty in our behalf; the Father, everlasting in
his mercy: is it too much to think that he is given
to us? Oh, that this war-torn earth would be
kissed by the Prince of Peace. Come, Lord Jesus!

Lifeline

> ...And everyone who calls on the name
> of the LORD will be saved;... Joel 2:32 NIV

"Saved? Saved from what?" That question
often comes from people who are offered salvation by someone who shares Christ with them.
These people, if they reject, are "calling upon"
their own strengths and righteousness. Unfortunately, it is often too late before they discover
that their resources are inadequate.

"Lord, be merciful to me, a sinner." That is
the cry that always receives a positive answer

from God. Always. To everyone. Is there any promise greater than this? No! So, I will call on him.

Shoulder to Shoulder

> Then will I purify the lips of the peoples, that all of them may call on the name of the LORD and serve him shoulder to shoulder.
> Zephaniah 3:9 NIV

Anyone who knows he is a product of grace can work beside another product of grace. No one who calls on the Name of the Lord can stand higher than another. If we call on his Name, we work side by side, shoulder to shoulder and are glad to do it. And, "Since through God's mercy we have this ministry, we do not lose heart." (2 Corinthians 4:1)

Hall of Fame

> Then they that feared the LORD spake often one to another: and the LORD hearkened, and heard it, and a book of remembrance was written before him for them that feared the LORD, and that thought upon his name. Malachi 3:16

If you run faster, leap higher, hit harder and do other amazing physical exploits, you have a good chance to be in some hall of fame. However, it becomes only a pittance of remembrance.

Soon, only your pictures and some mementos will remain. The hall of remembrance actually becomes a hall of forgetfulness. When the last person who actually saw you perform is dead, you also are a forgotten person.

Another hall of fame exists: a true hall of remembrance. The God who saw you play on this field of life does not die—you will never be forgotten. In fact, the scroll of remembrance for you will remain in the presence of God just so he remembers you always. What do you have to do to get into this hall of fame? Simply fear the Lord and talk with each other. What a winner a spiritual athlete is!

God does have a forgetter though—a hall of forgetfulness. He forgets our sins.

Dance, Soul, dance.

Cavorting Calves

> But for you who revere my name, the sun of righteousness will rise with healing in its wings. And you will go out and leap like calves released from the stall. Malachi 4:2 NIV

Dancing in the streets accompanies many freedom celebrations. When wars are over, whole nations will erupt into dancing. It may last for a day or even a week, but then the dancing is over and we return to the realities of work.

God has ordained an eternal dance for his children—a dance that will never end. He also described its steps. I remember from my days on a farm the freedom kicks of released calves. They seem forced to stretch every muscle in their bodies. Freedom plays the heartstrings of all God's creatures. But our dance, this fringe benefit of grace, is no temporary freedom from which we must finally settle down. Not only are our sins permanently forgiven, but healing arises and our souls leap in their new freedom. No soul is so light as the one whose burden of sin has been removed. "It is for freedom that Christ has set us free." (Galatians 5:1) Leap, Soul, leap!

Pick A Name

> And she shall bring forth a son, and thou shalt call his name JESUS: for he shall save his people from their sins.
> Matthew 1:21

Naming children can be very significant and stressful. "Who will we name the child after?" is the question of many families. Names we like or names that sound good generally take precedence over other "traditional" forms of naming after family members. Imagine the power of the conversation that might have occurred between Jesus and his caretaker father, Joseph:

"What does my name mean?"

"It means 'YHWH saves.'"

"Who named me?"

"YHWH did."

"Why did he name me that?"

"Because you are going to save your people from their sin."

"Why was he the one who named me?"

"Because you are his son."

Do you suppose Jesus thought often about this? A given in his life to shape his future. Call him "Yahshua, YHWH saves, Jesus."

National Hope

> In his name the nations will put their hope. Matthew 12:21 NIV

The public goal of politics seems to be "Throw the rascals out." It doesn't take long to discover that whichever party leads a nation, whatever man takes its reigns, he will surely be there just long enough for everyone to know that he failed. Only distant history with its merciful forgetfulness will ascribe any greatness or success. There doesn't seem to be much hope.

Often, as I journey, the situation I see in some countries causes me to despair of any chance that their poverty or ignorance or disease will ever be erased. Little hope exists.

The Communist world crumbled. They did their best to make their system work. Time made Communism a laughing stock. Their best hopes crashed. Not just the Communist world, the *whole* world is also crumbling around us. Uncontrollable crime permeates every status of our society from the streets to the corporations to the government. Drug lords are stronger and richer than the countries of their origin. Not one social program, not one, has been able to turn human nature around. Greed is our first name, our middle name and our family name.

Hope exists, though. One king has proven himself faithful. He waits for our eyes to turn to him.

Who Does He Think He Is?

"Isn't this the carpenter's son? Isn't his mother's name Mary, and aren't his brothers James, Joseph, Simon and Judas?" Matthew 13:55 NIV

I include this verse because of its implications. What the crowds were saying is that Jesus was a person of *no big name*. For someone less than elite, this is an expected complaint. Isn't this just an ordinary man? Isn't he just like us? Wasn't he here among us for thirty years? What is so special about him? Why should we listen to him?

The complaint that he was common provides an unparalleled witness to the Scripture and the reality of Jesus. "The Word became *flesh* and dwelt among us." "Emmanuel—God with us."

Yes, he is just like us. Yes, he has walked the same roads we have. He has lived with sibling rivalry just like us. He is "touched" with the feeling of our infirmities. The list goes on. What other complaints do you have against this "ordinary" man—this man of "no name?" He eats with sinners? He touches lepers? He welcomes children? Yes, go on....

Children Allowed

> "And whoever welcomes a little child like this in my name welcomes me."
> Matthew 18:5 NIV

A mark of our deteriorating times is how we are treating children. Abuse and abortion abound. Where is Jesus during all of this? He is feeling every violent act, being discarded in the refuse of every interrupted pregnancy, walking in the loneliness of every child with a key to an empty house. I wish we could figure out a better way to welcome him.

Name Droppers

> For many shall come in my name, saying, I am Christ; and shall deceive many.
> Matthew 24:5

We love to attach ourselves to great names. No one would ever come in the name of Stalin, Hitler, or Idi Amin. No, we steal from the virtue of a great name. We minor-leaguers offer hope when we have none. We are filled with anxieties and try to offer peace. We try to conquer the world and can't even conquer ourselves. We even call our institutions "Christian" while relentless fighting goes on among us. We are "deceivers all" whenever we try to elevate any of our institutions or denominations to "deliverer" status.

A friend told me a story that troubles me. It is a bit harsh, but forgive me as I relate it to you. Someone asked him in response to a time of boasting about and promoting his denomination, "Do you believe your church is *The* Bride of Christ?" When he answered, "No," the man responded, "That would make your church a prostitute, then." My friend felt the pain of this dilemma and resolved to have a larger view of the body of Christ and be less parochial about his own little exclusive group.

Fill It to the Brim

> For whosoever shall give you a cup of water to drink in my name, because ye belong to Christ, verily I say unto you, he shall not lose his reward. Mark 9:41

How delightfully easy it is to serve the Lord. Opportunities are as close as the water fountain. Ministry is as close as the nearest thirsty person. Amazing. And we only have to do it in *his* Name. Why, that can make every one of us to be ministers. Hey, this is a simple way to guarantee our future reward. Now, where is my cup?

Surprise, Surprise, Surprise

> Blessed are ye, when men shall hate you, and when they shall separate you from their company, and shall reproach you, and cast out your name as evil, for the Son of man's sake. Luke 6:22

Some things surprise me. Why would anyone want to hate me because of Jesus? Why should they reject my name when he was so great? What could pervert the heart of man to do such an evil thing as hate someone because of Christ? It seems absurd, yet it happens. Obviously, Satan is real and active in the world. Funny that we should pat Satan on the head and call him "cute" at Halloween. Another surprise. God blesses us when men do such evil things to us because we follow Jesus. I know Satan wasn't counting on that!

Speed Demons

> And the seventy returned again with joy, saying, Lord, even the devils are subject unto us through thy name. Luke 10:17

Demons have little else to do in the presence of the Name of Jesus except to say, "Goodbye." Power was in the hands of the apostles and on their lips. They enjoyed that power, but Jesus quickly short-circuited it. He informed this power-drunk crew that salvation was the cup of joy, not power. (Luke 10:20) Hmm. That makes Luke 10:20 one of the most disobeyed verses in scripture, doesn't it?

Lamb Chops

> But before all these, they shall lay their hands on you, and persecute you, delivering you up to the synagogues, and into prisons, being brought before kings and rulers for my name's sake. Luke 21:12

Synagogues, kings, governors, law-enforcers—sounds like all the power centers we ever wanted to speak to. Take on the Name of Jesus, be sent as a lamb among wolves, and you will find yourself among the powerful—being persecuted, of course, but you will be there in the halls of power. I wonder what they are afraid of—these power centers—that would cause them to seek us out to persecute us? "Baaa." I love God's sense of humor.

Only One Way

> ...and repentance and forgiveness of sins will be preached in his name to all nations, beginning at Jerusalem. Luke 24:47

> Whoever believes in him is not condemned, but whoever does not believe

> stands condemned already because he has not believed in the name of God's one and only Son. John 3:18

> But these are written that you may believe that Jesus is the Christ, the Son of God, and that by believing you may have life in his name. John 20:31

> And everyone who calls on the name of the Lord will be saved. Acts 2:21

> Salvation is found in no one else, for there is no other name under heaven given to men by which we must be saved. Acts 4:12 NIV

Actually, there is no other Name in which repentance and forgiveness *can* be preached. A fundamental statement of Buddhism is that "Buddha does not save." So long, Buddha. Mohammed has only toil, no grace. So long, Mohammed. Hinduism doesn't even know what it has or whether there is anything to offer, so it seeks appeasement. So long, Krishna of the Hindus. Welcome, Jesus.

Friendly Reminder

> But the Comforter, which is the Holy Ghost, whom the Father will send in my name, he shall teach you all things, and bring all things to your remembrance, whatsoever I have said unto you. John 14:26

God must have known how good a forgetter I have, so he sends the Holy Spirit to bring the words of Jesus back to me. That puts us in a very good position—rather safe: Jesus teaches—the Holy Spirit reminds. In fact, this knowledge can give us some good basics to believe: You can be sure the Holy Spirit is active in your life if Jesus keeps coming back to mind. Why would anyone want to be without the Holy Spirit?

Poor But Powerful

> Then Peter said, Silver and gold have I none; but such as I have give I thee: In the name of Jesus Christ of Nazareth rise up and walk. Acts 3:6
> And his name through faith in his name hath made this man strong, whom ye see and know: yea, the faith which is by him hath given him this perfect soundness in the presence of you all. 16

You can't give what you don't have. All Peter and John had was Jesus. They gave him. All we seem to have now is silver and gold. We give...?

The religious leaders who disapproved of what Peter and John had done (seems ludicrous doesn't it) moved quickly to the core of the problem—in whose name (authority) did they do this? These men knew what Jesus was like. Why shouldn't they heal the sick. That is like Jesus, isn't it?

Strange Happiness

> And they departed from the presence of the council, rejoicing that they were counted worthy to suffer shame for his name. Acts 5:41
> But the Lord said unto him, Go thy way: for he is a chosen vessel unto me, to bear my name before the Gentiles, and kings, and the children of Israel: 9:15

These men find happiness in strange ways. Jesus had said "Rejoice and be exceeding glad" when you are persecuted, but hardly any of us actually believe that verse. When I am persecuted, I have a world-class pity-party. Paul was given a vision that included the things he would have to suffer. For some reason, he was not too upset by that prospect. He even gloried in the violence he would have to suffer in each city he approached. We even find Paul and Silas singing songs in the middle of the night in a dungeon. Remarkable.

I am not to the point that I want to pray for persecution to come my way, but I certainly do want to be in touch with what made those men sing.

Naming the Family

> For this cause I bow my knees unto the Father of our Lord Jesus Christ, Of whom the whole family in heaven and earth is named,.... Ephesians 3:14,15

Of course we are brothers and sisters. You see, we all have the same last name, I AM. Maybe that is why we favor each other so much and have so many similar actions. Maybe that is why we are so embarrassed when someone among us shames our family name. Something spiritually genetic has shaped the part of us that is eternal, and we are glad that it has.

Our Father's name informs us that he is who he is—in him there is no darkness or dishonesty. His name informs us that he is here now and will be with us forever and will be sufficient for us. Thus, we make some statements about the family:

Our family name "I AM" marks us as honest.

Our family name "I AM" marks us as present.

Our family name "I AM" marks us as enduring.

Living up to this name requires more than I can physically supply. Thank God it is genetic, spiritually.

Top Name

> Therefore God exalted him to the highest place and gave him the name that is above every name, that at the name of Jesus every knee should bow, in heaven and on earth and under the earth,.....
> Philippians 2:9-10 NIV

What preceeds the "Therefore?" Jesus had successfully revealed the nature of the Father through his own life and had abandoned use of physical force to make us disciples, had purposed to use heavenly means to achieve heavenly goals, had made himself of no reputation, had taken on the nature of a servant and the likeness of man, had humbled himself and been obedient at the price of death on the cross. Every one of these traits represented failure in the eyes of the world. But look at the results of obedience to the nature of the Father—exaltation.

He is the worthy one. I gladly bow my knee before him.

Doing It His Way

> And whatsoever ye do in word or deed, do all in the name of the Lord Jesus, giving thanks to God and the Father by him. Colossians 3:17

Now that I belong to him, I relinquish all rights except to act in his Name. I go to work in the Name of Jesus. I married my wife in the Name of Jesus. I raise my children in the Name of Jesus. I purchase groceries in the Name of Jesus. I vote in the Name of Jesus. I watch television in the Name of Jesus (somewhat difficult to do). I am glad I can do it that way. The interesting question is, "What is the option in life to acting in the Name of Jesus?"

Passport Please

> If anyone's name was not found written
> in the book of life, he was thrown into the
> lake of fire. Revelation 20:15 NIV

The Bible does not straddle the fence. Either we are followers of Jesus and can expect to enjoy Heaven with him or else we are not followers of Jesus and our end is the lake of fire. Many people mock and say "How can a loving God throw people into a lake of fire just because they don't know him?" However, the real question is, "How can anyone hear of the love of God and not become a follower?" I don't know. I simply don't know.

Headlines

> And I looked, and, lo, a Lamb stood on
> the mount Sion, and with him an hundred
> forty and four thousand, having his Fa-
> ther's name written in their foreheads.
> Revelation 14:1
> And they shall see his face; and his
> name shall be in their foreheads. 22:4

The forehead, symbol of all our higher thoughts and decision making, is the proper place for the Name of our God. I cannot help but exult at the thought that, someday, his Name/Nature will occupy my thoughts and decisions. At that time, it will be an effort (hopefully impossible) to be anything except like him.

At this prospect a brass band marches through my heart. Blessed be the Name of the Lord.

Glory

As we continue meditating on the Nature of our Lord, keep in mind that we have established that "Name" and "Glory" have the same definition. You can see in this series on the word "Glory" that the definitions and applications are interchangeable.

Set Apart

> And there I will meet with the children of Israel, and the tabernacle shall be sanctified by my glory. Exodus 29:43

The Glory of the Lord is defined as the "essence of his being." The "essence of his being" is also described in the meaning of his Name, thus one can almost use the words "Name" and "Glory" interchangeably. To be sanctified is to be set apart for special use.

Now that we have our definitions behind us, the verse in this meditation begins to focus very clearly. The presence of his Glory (essence-nature) sanctified (set apart) the tabernacle. We have exhibited in these pages that his Name-Glory is his Compassion, Grace, Longsuffering, Faithfulness and Forgiveness. You can be sure that any place/person where this compassion resides, will be vastly different—inescapably set apart from all other things. If you know of someone who is very compassionate and gracious or slow to anger or forgiving, chances are that person stands out from the crowd. You would quickly say, "that person is different."

Another definition—a theological one: We know that now, God does not dwell in temples made with hands. We have, by his declaration, become his temple; therefore, whenever you see in the Bible a place where God dwells, translate it into New Testament terms—our bodies. Now, *we* are his tabernacle. That brings this verse to its joyous conclusion: We, bathed in his compassion and grace and forgiveness, are now set apart for his use. It doesn't get any better than that.

Cloud Cover

> Then a cloud covered the tent of the congregation, and the glory of the LORD filled the tabernacle. And Moses was not able to enter into the tent of the congregation, because the cloud abode thereon, and the glory of the LORD filled the tabernacle.
> Exodus 40:34,35

The thoughts in the verses above connect to another such intervention of the Glory of God, this time at the dedication of the temple:

So that the priests could not stand to minister by reason of the cloud: for the glory of the LORD had filled the house of God. 2 Chronicles 5:14

Now when Solomon had made an end of praying, the fire came down from heaven, and consumed the burnt offering and the sacrifices; and the glory of the LORD filled the house. And the priests could not enter into the house of the LORD because the glory of the LORD had filled the LORD's house. And when all the children of Israel saw how the fire came down, and the glory of the LORD upon the house, they bowed themselves with their faces to the ground upon the pavement, and worshiped, and praised the LORD, saying, For he is good; for his mercy endureth for ever. 7:1-3

What was it about the Glory of God that would stop all human effort? Moses and Solomon could not enter the house of God and the priests could not minister. Why would the Glory of God do that? Is his Glory some strange glow that would melt the face of a Nazi as Hollywood would have us believe? Is it just a cloud?

Now that we understand his Glory to be the same as his compassionate, merciful nature, we can quickly understand what was happening in the tabernacle and temple. In the presence of overwhelming grace there is nothing that we humans can do but receive. We cannot enter, we cannot minister, we can only receive. That is hard for an arrogant human like myself. I want to earn; I want to be good enough; I want to forge ahead. But my loving, giving God says, "Be still! Receive!" Oh, to learn to receive.

There is only one thing I can do in the presence of such Glory—I can fall on my face and worship!

Loud Speaker

> Declare his glory among the heathen;
> his marvelous works among all nations.
> 1 Chronicles 16:24

We cannot find a better condensation of the meaning of evangelism. Declare his compassion; declare his grace; declare his longsufferingness; declare his love and faithfulness; declare his forgiveness. The world does not long to hear about his judgment. The world is not hungry for more guilt. The world hungers to know, "Is God there and does he love us?" Declare it!

The anointing of Jesus confirmed this approach as coming to "proclaim the season of God's favor." How else can we fulfill the covenant to "bless all nations" unless we declare his Glory and marvelous works.

Good Bye, Glory

> She named the child Ichabod, saying,
> The glory is departed from Israel: because
> the ark of God was taken.... 1 Samuel 4:21

The Ark of the Covenant was all Israel had. Their military had always been small and weak, winning victories only by the miraculous intervention of YHWH. Spiritually, at the time of this passage, they had nothing. Eli had been a terrible chief priest, and his sons, Hophni and Phinehas, multiplied the corruption. The only great act of Eli apparently had been to tell Samuel to say "hineni" or "I am here," and then to listen to God.

Now, in the face of foreign threat their only hope was that the Ark would bring them luck. They had nothing else. It appears that the Ark had been reduced from the presence of God to a mere talisman. The nation's devotion to God had been abandoned because of the dubious influence of their clergy.

So, against the overwhelming odds, they brought their only treasure into the midst of their troops. Emotion ran high. The shout, heard by the Philistines, struck terror in their hearts. They knew of the power of YHWH. Like cornered beasts, the Philistines fought beyond their ability, and the battle was over. Israel lost. The Ark belonged to the Philistines.

Eli, now 98 years old and quite fat, fell over, broke his neck and died. Nothing left to live for. But the real story was yet to be heard. One person understood the seriousness of the situation—the wife of Phinehas. She was pregnant, and, at the news, entered into labor and delivered a son—a son she did not want—a son she ignored.

Finally, she screamed a name and wailed a despair, "Ichabod." The Glory has departed. Gone was their door of compassion, grace, long-suffering, love, faithfulness, forgiveness. The last treasure they had, the *only* treasure they had, was gone. Ichabod. Grace was gone. The only thing left was the Law. Misery. Ichabod. The Glory is gone.

Ichabod still lives. When we build a system or institution that depends on works or develops a law or does not live in grace and forgiveness—write "Ichabod" on it. When our group chooses to focus on issues and traditions, not Jesus and the Word, write "Ichabod" on it. Ichabod has been around too long. How can we rid ourselves of Ichabod?

Repent, then write "Glory."

Idol Blues

And the Philistines took the ark of God, and brought it from Ebenezer unto Ashdod. When the Philistines took the ark of God, they brought it into the house of Dagon, and set it by Dagon.

And when they of Ashdod arose early on the morrow, behold, Dagon was fallen upon his face to the earth before the ark of the LORD. And they took Dagon, and set him in his place again. And when they arose early on the morrow morning, behold, Dagon was fallen upon his face to the ground before the ark of the LORD; and the head of Dagon and both the palms of his hands were cut off upon the threshold; only the stump of Dagon was left to him.

Therefore neither the priests of Dagon, nor any that come into Dagon's house, tread on the threshold of Dagon in Ashdod unto this day. 1 Samuel 5:1-5

Israel didn't understand the Ark and neither did the Philistines. Most people understand the rules but don't understand grace. They understand "symbols" but not the "Presence."

In a hilarious act, the Philistines sat the Ark, the "Glory," at the feet of Dagon, their idol. The next morning Dagon was down on his face. The score in this contest was now the Ark—1, Dagon—0. You would think the Philistines would understand, but ,"No!" They put their "god" back upright (He needed all the help he could get), but the next morning Dagon was fallen again and his head and hands were broken off and lying on the threshold. The score now? Ark—2, Dagon—0. Did the Philistines understand? No! Now, they became more superstitious and would not step on the threshold any more. I imagine they tried to find a better "god-maker" to craft a sturdier idol. Ah well, they don't make gods like they used to.

Unfortunately, Dagon seems to persist in our lives. Any plan, system, institution that we shape and then try to graft God into—watch it fall. Hopefully, we will "give in" to the Glory rather than try to improve our institutions, our Dagons.

What Do You See in the Clouds?

> The heavens declare the glory of God;
> and the firmament sheweth his handiwork.
> Psalms 19:1

David wrote another such psalm that spoke of his Glory contained in Chronicles:

> Thine, O LORD, is the greatness, and the power, and the glory, and the victory, and the majesty: for all that is in the heaven and in the earth is thine; thine is the king-dom, O LORD, and thou art exalted as head above all. 1 Chronicles 29:11

If one eats the bread of harvested grain;
If one plucks and eats a sweetened fruit;
If one watches wounds heal;
If one gazes at a distant star;
One can know the grace of God.

What arrogant heart ever dares say, "I made this. I am a god."? What prattling human being ever dares place himself on the throne of his life? Did he make the grain to grow? Did he form and name the stars? No! Thine, O Lord, is the Glory.

Great Pretenders

> Lift up your heads, O ye gates; and be ye lifted up, ye everlasting doors; and the King of glory shall come in. Who is this King of glory? The LORD strong and mighty, the LORD mighty in battle. Lift up your heads, O ye gates; even lift them up, ye everlasting doors; and the King of glory shall come in. Who is this King of glory? The LORD of hosts, he is the King of glory. Selah. Psalms 24:7-10

The pretenders to this throne are many. Your employer would like you to think that his company is everything you need. Your pay check would like to say to you that money is all you need. You expect your spouse or friend to meet your needs. You expect drugs or alcohol or vacations to restore you. Pretenders, all! The only supplier of compassion, grace and forgiveness is the King of Glory. If we ask anything or anyone to supply what the King is there to supply, we have asked them to be what they cannot be.

If you find yourself in need of compassion, forgiveness or grace, seek the fulfillment first at the top of the hierarchy. Seek the King. Ask of others only what they can truly supply.

Flesh Party

> Not unto us, O LORD, not unto us, but unto thy name give glory, for thy mercy, and for thy truth's sake. Psalms 115:1

> I am the LORD: that is my name: and my glory will I not give to another, neither my praise to graven images. Isaiah 42:8

> Thus saith the LORD, Let not the wise man glory in his wisdom, neither let the mighty man glory in his might, let not the rich man glory in his riches: But let him that glorieth glory in this, that he understandeth and knoweth me, that I am the LORD which exercise lovingkindness, judgment, and righteousness, in the earth: for in these things I delight, saith the LORD. Jeremiah 9:23,24

My flesh loves glory. I like it when I read good things about myself in the newspaper. I am proud when my books get good reviews. I love glowing introductions before I speak. Ah, my flesh revels in it. The problem is: in my flesh there dwells no good thing.

Let me have a good job and I will look down on the unemployed. Let me have a good house and I will resent lesser houses in my neighborhood. Let me have good children and I will criticize those who don't. Let me have good looks and I will avoid those who don't. Let me have strength and I will overpower the weak. My flesh is not a candidate for corruption—it *is* the corrupter. But God will not let flesh win. Flesh is a thief and a robber. It deceives through a scheme called "feel good."

As far as I can see in the Bible, the only area left to us for "braggin' rights" is that we know God. No achievement of mine is worth the price of a piece of paper to honor it. No honor is worth the time it takes to receive it. No fame is worth a muscle's twitch of effort. Vanity! All of it.

However, if you know God, Brag!

Fleshing Out God

> And the Word was made flesh, and dwelt among us, and we beheld his glory, the glory as of the only begotten of the Father, full of grace and truth. John 1:14

It is the belief of many people, including me, that the Angel that spoke to Moses from the burning bush and that wrestled with Jacob was a pre-fleshly appearance of Jesus (a theophany). Good evidence exists that any fleshly appearance of God to mankind is the person of Jesus. In other words, Jesus is always the face of God and the interface with man.

Evidence that Jesus is both the revelation of God and also *is* the God of Glory is so strong that it seems undeniable. From the first moments of God's interface with man in the Old Testament (That must have been Jesus himself) to the incredible John 1:18 that places Jesus as both God and revealer (intermediary, mediator) we are surrounded with proof. Listen to what John says about him in our next meditation:

Now You See Him

> No one has ever seen God, but God the One and Only, who is at the Father's side, has made him known. John 1:18 NIV

The quickest way to judge if a people have strayed from the God of the Bible is to learn how they view Jesus. If they reduce Jesus to something less than the Only Begotten, Only Redeemer, Only Revealer of YHWH, then you can be sure that error will be compounded in what they teach. That is why one is safest in his standing, surest in his walk when he chooses to search out the nature of Jesus and judge all things accordingly.

Now, in John 1:14, the writer joins the ranks of Moses in beholding the Glory of God in the person of Jesus. Just so you can be sure that this is God, he even describes what that Glory is—full of grace and truth. This is merely a condensation, a shorthand expression, of the great declaration of his Name/Glory—compassionate, gracious, slow to anger, abounding in mercy and faithfulness, maintaining love to thousands, forgiving wickedness, rebellion and sin.

Though Moses received the meaning of his Name and description of his Glory, the experiencing of that Glory and full revelation waited until later. Moses was only permitted to see the back of God—only a glimpse. The face waited for Jesus. Consequently, John overflows with the joy that must have made Abraham leap when he saw this day:

Mirror, Mirror

> From the fullness of his grace we have all received one blessing after another. For the law was given through Moses; grace and truth came through Jesus Christ. John 1:16,17 NIV

> But we all, with open face beholding as in a glass the glory of the Lord, are changed into the same image from glory to glory, even as by the Spirit of the Lord. 2 Corinthians 3:18

The progression of hope in this verse is almost too good to be true.

1. We expose ourselves to God—open our faces or remove our veils.

2. God shines his Glory (compassion, grace, forgiveness) down upon us to redeem, not condemn.

3. We reflect his Glory—show that we have received that grace and consequently shine it on others.

4. We are being changed. Notice that it actually is a passive statement. The change is happening to us; we are not doing it ourselves. That is very encouraging to me, since I have learned that I cannot change myself.

5. The goal of our change is the likeness of Jesus. We are being made over to be like him. Can you think of a better goal? This is too good.

6. We go from Glory to Glory. His grace does not diminish, it is made new every day. The more we know ourselves and can thus reveal ourselves more to God, the more he shines his grace down on us—ever-increasing Glory.

7. The Holy Spirit is at work in us. This change is not our doing. Praise be to God!

So, if you find some area of your life you cannot conquer, expose (confess) it to God and he will shine his grace (Glory) down on you and change you to be more and more like himself. What a deal!

Under the Spotlight

> For God, who commanded the light to shine out of darkness, hath shined in our hearts to give the light of the knowledge of the glory of God in the face of Jesus Christ.
> 2 Corinthians 4:6

Moses asked to see the Glory of God. God responded that he would proclaim (explain) his name and let Moses catch a glimpse of his back but that he could not see his face. Moses possessed the definition of the Name of God in words, but not the experience of that definition. Now, in Jesus, the Face, the full definition, the expression, the experience of all that is God comes to us. Now we see his Face. Indeed, it is full of Glory (grace).

God had told Moses that to see his face was to die. They did not die when they saw Jesus? Why? Well, Jesus did the dying for them so they could see the face of God and live.

Glory, Glory, Glory

To the *praise of the glory* of his grace, wherein he hath made us accepted in the beloved. Ephesians 1:6

That we should be to the *praise of his glory,* who first trusted in Christ. 12

Which is the earnest of our inheritance until the redemption of the purchased possession, unto the *praise of his glory.* 14

The eyes of your understanding being enlightened; that ye may know what is the hope of his calling, and what the *riches of the glory* of his inheritance in the saints.. 18

That he would grant you, according to the *riches of his glory,* to be strengthened with might by his Spirit in the inner man;... 3:16 (My emphasis)

Suppose you took a room full of Christians and had them relate the times they have experienced the compassion, grace, faithfulness or forgiveness of God. How long do you think it might take before the whole room would have finished with their stories? You could spend years together! That is one reason I believe in Heaven. There, we will have the time to know and be known.

Paul records in the first verses of Ephesians the incredible journey of a Christian—we are blessed, chosen, predestined, graced, redeemed, forgiven, included, sealed, and given purpose. All of this given to us so we can praise his Glory. Is it any wonder that we call our times together in church "worship" services? It is impossible to walk through the list of the facets of his Glory without saying, "This is good news."

The further good news is that this Glory is not depleted. No moment of great redemption in your life ever depleted the amount you might need later. Even the deposit ("earnest," Ephesians 1:13,14) guaranteeing our inheritance, which is almost more than we can receive, left no dent in the stored riches of his Glory. Whatever praise you can give, give freely that his Glory might be known. Whatever strength you need, dip often into his riches so you will know how much is there.

Voice Print of God

In these last days he has spoken to us by his Son, whom he appointed heir of all things, and through whom he made the universe. The Son is the radiance of God's glory and the exact representation of his being, sustaining all things by his powerful word. After he had provided purification for sins, he sat down at the right hand of the Majesty in heaven. Hebrews 1:2,3 NIV

Here is further indication why it must have
been Jesus who walked past Moses on the
mountain and why he couldn't have looked at
his face at that time. Jesus was the radiance
(brightness, expression) of God's Glory.

Heaven had a choice to make: who can we
send who will properly represent compassion,
grace, longsuffering, love, faithfulness, forgiveness? He must be exact and true representation;
he cannot vary one iota. No course correction
can occur in the midst of the representation and
no damage control must be necessary after the
presentation. Heaven's choice was surely the
Son. Only he is the "exact representation."

So do not look or wait for some additional
revelation. Do not try for some deeper moment
yet to come. The completeness is here. Jesus has
come. The Glory shines! (See "Face" Gen. 32:30.)
May his Glory fill all the earth as the water cov-
ers the sea!

The Face

As you have observed throughout this book, God has revealed himself in defining his Name and his Glory. God has chosen to complete the revelation of himself by letting us see his Face in Jesus Christ. Because of the powerful symbolism and the actuality of "Face" it is appropriate that we turn our eyes toward him even as he turns his Face toward us.

Hide Me, Quickly

> Behold, thou hast driven me out this day from the face of the earth; and from thy face shall I be hid; and I shall be a fugitive and a vagabond in the earth; and it shall come to pass, that every one that findeth me shall slay me. Genesis 4:14

As history goes, only a blip of time separated paradise from disaster. Eden was a time of meeting; post-Eden (the earth as we know it) is a time of parting. First, Adam parted with Eden, then parted with ease, then parted with Abel and finally parted with Cain. But the saddest parting is of Cain from the Face of God. His succession of choices hides him from compassionate interaction with God. How sad to have known his gaze of grace and to lose it. Finally, he loses what

may have been the last remaining sign of innocence—his inability to hide his guilt. God must
have performed some primal lobotomy on Cain
so that his face could now be made to reflect
something different from his inner state.

Jump to the distant future and we must now
have juries and trials to hopefully determine
guilt or innocence, because now the face has
joined in the big lie of deception. Humility, which
simply portrays the truth about ourselves, had
suffered a defeat from which it could not recover.
This was one of mankind's darkest days.

Now, man could only hope that a restorer, a
healer, a messiah, a Jesus, would come.

I Saw God

> So Jacob called the place Peniel, saying,
> "It is because I saw God face to face, and
> yet my life was spared." Genesis 32:30 NIV

Despondency must have stalked Jacob that
night when he heard the news that his brother
Esau was waiting for him with an army. What
could he do now? He sent his family one direc-
tion, his goods another direction, gifts over to
his brother; and, that night, Jacob was alone
with himself. What a thing to be alone with when
you are a trickster like Jacob. I once had a phi-
losopher ask me, "Have you ever knocked at
your own door and found yourself not home?"
That was Jacob's status—lights on, nobody
home.

In the middle of his despondency, a messenger from God appears. Indeed, a "wrestling" messenger from God. This scene I hope God will let me see on "instant replay" when I get to Heaven. I want to know what caused Jacob to decide to take on the wrestler. The match was not easy. Wrestling in college or Olympic competition usually lasts about nine minutes per match. At the end of those nine minutes, the contestants are completely exhausted. Jacob and the Angel wrestled all night! And nobody won!

It was the greatest match Jacob ever lost. When he surrendered as is indicated by his asking the Angel to bless him (showing the Angel's superior strength), to his amazement, the Angel gifted him with a new name. No longer would he have to carry the name that loosely translates as "dirty, sneaky thief." From now on he would be called "Israel, Prince of God," because he had wrestled with God and man and won. He won? How? He surrendered.

In the conversation that continued, Jacob knew that this encounter had been with God himself. He had seen the Face and had been spared.

Evidently, Jacob's persistent opponent that night was none other than Jesus himself and Jacob sensed that eternity struggled with him in that desert. That sense brought about Jacob's most brilliant act—his surrender. At that point, he discovered life's greatest secret: If you want to win with God, give up!

Many of us wrestle with God until we are exhausted, even crippled (as happened to Jacob), when all we have to do to win is to give up. Let us surrender quickly.

Bring Your Brother

> And Judah spake unto him, saying, The man did solemnly protest unto us, saying, Ye shall not see my face, except your brother be with you. Genesis 43:3

Judah reports to his dad, Israel (Jacob), on the trip to Egypt and the demands of Joseph, although they did not yet know it was Joseph. Joseph is often considered an Old Testament "type" of Christ in his consistent life and deliverance role. The demand he makes of his brothers sounds so much like one Jesus would make—If you want to see my face, bring your brother.

In John 17, Jesus, praying a "high priestly" prayer, repeats a prayer phrase five times, "Father, that they may be one." The desire of Jesus for brotherly love is unequivocal. There is no option. The Gospel is not independent of relationships. If we want to see our Lord's Face, we must bring our brother.

One of the songs of the singing group called "Love Song" of the Jesus Movement of the 1970's said it well, "...use your own two hands. With one reach out to Jesus, and with the other, bring a friend."

An interesting side note exists here, also. Although, on the surface, it appears that Joseph is merely testing his brothers, it could also be said that Joseph was toying with them, mistreating them. This abusive action is inappropriate to anyone who has a forgiving spirit. It was Judah who went into action to rescue the scene and eventually offered himself for his brother because he could not face his father if Benjamin did not return with them.

Perhaps at that moment, the decision was made as to which line the Messiah would come through. The logical ancestral line would flow through Joseph, but instead Judah was chosen. Maybe when Judah threw himself in as "redeemer" in place of Benjamin, God decided that Judah's was the spirit that was to continue. Just possibly.

Don't Try to Box with God

"...I will set my face against..."
Leviticus 17:10, 20:3, 20:5, 20:6, 26:17

The list of actions that will cause God to set his "Face" against someone is gruesome:

1. Someone who eats blood
2. Someone who sacrifices his children to Molech (an idol)
3. Someone who worships Molech
4. Someone who turns to mediums and spiritists (the occult)

The result is equally gruesome: that person would be defeated by his enemies, ruled by someone he hated and would fearfully flee even when he wasn't pursued (paranoia).

The actions listed above are obviously actions against Jesus and would cause the wonderful accepting Face of God to turn against us. Could it be that the violence, abortion, occultism and drug use of our day are beginning to take their toll? This should move us to increased prayer and compassion for our generation so that the words of the following meditation will apply.

Son Shine

> The LORD bless you and keep you; the LORD make his face shine upon you and be gracious to you; the LORD turn his face toward you and give you peace. Numbers 6:24-26 NIV

Little did the sons of Aaron know as they pronounced this blessing that they were asking God to shine Jesus upon the people. To turn his Face (Jesus) toward them was to issue them Grace and Truth. What a powerful blessing. May it pour from our lips.

About Face!

> If my people, which are called by my
> name, shall humble themselves, and pray,
> and seek my face, and turn from their
> wicked ways; then will I hear from heaven,
> and will forgive their sin, and will heal their
> land. 2 Chronicles 7:14

We have the option of turning our backs on God. We can go our own way—indeed, we do! Our self-ways devastate friends and family far beyond ourselves. Our land is damaged and sickened. Our hearts are hardened. We do evil things to one another. We become proud and arrogant and greedy. We think we are the source of any prosperity we have.

To receive from the Lord always implies and often demands a repentance, a turning of directions. It is only logical. His Face was always turned toward us, but our backs were toward him. Now, we turn from our ways and go toward his Face. Such action humbles us but produces good fruit.

Oh, that the paths toward his Face were well worn!

Fooling Satan

> But put forth thine hand now, and touch all that he hath, and he will curse thee to thy face. Job 1:11

Satan certainly underestimated Job. Job may have been the most wise and righteous man recorded for us in the Old Testament. He knew who the source of his wealth was—not himself, but God. In spite of all the misery and misfortune, Job knew what God was like and he was determined to follow God with or without prosperity. Listen to his words:

> Though he slay me, yet will I trust in him:... 13:15
> But he knoweth the way that I take: when he hath tried me, I shall come forth as gold. My foot hath held his steps, his way have I kept, and not declined. Neither have I gone back from the commandment of his lips; I have esteemed the words of his mouth more than my necessary food. 23:10-12
> All the while my breath is in me, and the spirit of God is in my nostrils; My lips shall not speak wickedness, nor my tongue utter deceit. 27:3,4

Job knew and lived the nature of his God:

> Whoever heard me spoke well of me, and those who saw me commended me, because I rescued the poor who cried for help, and the fatherless who had none to assist

him. The man who was dying blessed me; I
made the widow's heart sing. I put on righteousness as my clothing; justice was my
robe and my turban.
    I was eyes to the blind and feet to the
lame. I was a father to the needy; I took up
the case of the stranger. I broke the fangs
of the wicked and snatched the victims
from their teeth. 29:11-17 NIV

I have thought of a new blessing we can pronounce upon one another: "May Satan always
underestimate you!"

Restoration Theology

Restore us, O LORD God Almighty;
make your face shine upon us, that we may
be saved. Psalm 80:3,7,19 NIV

God is the restorer of things. Our best cities
and strongest fortresses eventually become rub-
ble. Our best efforts at living are dogged with
mistake and misfortune. Our best efforts at res-
toration merely complicate the situation. We are
without the tools or materials to build. Enter,
God.

He restores what the cankerworm and pal-
merworm have eaten. Only he can accomplish
this task. Jesus broke up every funeral he at-
tended. He restored a dead son to his mother.

How many hopeless situations has he restored in our lives? Count them. It may take a
joyous while. How does God do this restoring?

He makes his Face (Jesus) to shine upon us. When that happens, there can be only one result—salvation!

Mercy! Out Front! Truth! Step Forward!

> Justice and judgment are the habitation of thy throne: mercy and truth go before thy face. Psalms 89:14

The Gospel of John declares that the "law came by Moses; grace and truth by Jesus Christ." Aha! Mercy and Truth—Grace and Truth: now we have further evidence that Jesus is the Face of God. When God wanted us to see himself, he gave us Jesus. Jesus affirms that statement by declaring that he and the Father were one.

Justice and judgment are frightening concepts when we consider our own guilt, and God knows that, so he has arranged to send mercy and truth in front of himself. If we see only his judgment, then we have turned our eyes away from his Face. Suddenly, the words of an old chorus take on new meaning:

"Turn your eyes upon Jesus.

Look full in his wonderful Face,

And the things of earth will grow strangely dim

In the light of his glory and grace."

Not a Flinch

> I gave my back to the smiters, and my cheeks to them that plucked off the hair: I hid not my face from shame and spitting. For the LORD God will help me; therefore shall I not be confounded: therefore have I set my face like a flint, and I know that I shall not be ashamed. Isaiah 50:6,7

This prophecy of Jesus overwhelms me. In the presence of mocking and spitting, the Face of grace shines ahead and says "peace and forgiveness." His grace is aggressive. He does not leave the mocker to spit in solitude, but makes his Face available for him to deride. So powerful is his grace that he sets it like flint to move ahead and accomplish redemption.

Peter tried hard to "rescue" Jesus from his suffering. In Matthew 16, Peter rebukes Jesus for thinking he will have to die. After all, he *is* the Messiah, isn't he? Jesus had to confront that temptation directly by saying, "Get behind me, Satan."

Smarting from his failure to stay awake for an apostolic prayer meeting in the garden, Peter, sword drawn, rushes to sever an ear from the head of Malchus, the chief priest's servant. If he can't support Jesus spiritually, he can, at least, rescue him physically. Again Peter hears the rebuke, "Put your sword away! Shall I not drink the cup the Father has given me?" (John 18:11)

Nothing Peter or anyone tried could sway this faithful Jesus from his appointment with death—no mocking, no spitting, no hair pulling, no well-meaning Apostle. He had set his Face like flint.

Awesome! What can I say?

Face Lift

> Take heed that ye despise not one of these little ones; for I say unto you, That in heaven their angels do always behold the face of my Father which is in heaven. Matthew 18:10

Seek your heights and titles and lofty achievements if you wish, but the gentle loving care of children brings you into the heart of God himself. A child always has the grace of the Father beaming toward him. Perhaps we should sit at the feet of the children.

No Mirrors in Heaven

> Now we see but a poor reflection as in a mirror; then we shall see face to face. Now I know in part; then I shall know fully, even as I am fully known. 1 Corinthians 13:12 NIV

What is the best our faces can do? Can they save? No. Do they offer grace? No. Can they see clearly? No. Do our eyes close in sleep? Yes. Do our ears fail to hear? Yes. Do our faces ever deceive? Yes. Does our discernment fail us? Yes.

What then is the best our faces can do? Fail. The only hope we have is that someday our face will see his Face. Then and only then can we know and be known.

Winners Circle

> And they shall see his face; and his name shall be in their foreheads.
> Revelation 22:4

The glorious conclusion: We will see his Face. Jesus will be the light of our city and the sun will no longer be needed. Grace will rule. Wickedness will be no more. Darkness will not exist where his Face is seen.

Stamped on our forehead will be his name:

Compassion
Grace
Slow to Anger
Abounding in love
Abounding in faithfulness
Maintaining love to the thousands
Forgiving wickedness
Forgiving rebellion
Forgiving sin

The forehead is a symbol of the location of our higher thinking, choices and judgments—a fitting place for his Name to be placed. In that day, with his Name lodged in us, the nature of our God will possess our higher judgments. We will automatically be like our God. To be otherwise would be unnatural. Then, our struggles to think his thoughts and match his nature will be over.

Someday, hopefully soon, that day will come when we will be forever in the presence of his Face and filled with his Glory and engraved with his Name. Come, Lord Jesus.

The following additional books and reference materials by Gayle Erwin are available from **Servant Quarters**, PO Box 219, Cathedral City, CA 92235. Complete catalog sent free. Phone 619-321-0077   FAX 619-324-3006

The Jesus Style

This book has been featured by Guidepost, Family Bookshelf and Word Book clubs, used as a textbook in colleges and seminaries and as a training manual in many churches. You will find yourself reading it more than once. Book and audiobook available, paperback, complete with a study guide.

The Spirit Style

This book breaks new ground in studying the Nature of God the Holy Spirit from the perspective of the Nature of Jesus. After reading this book, you will be able to rejoice over the action of God in your life today. Book and audiobook available. Published by Yahshua Publishing, Cathedral City, CA.

Video and Audio Tapes

Many hours of Erwin's unique and humorous but life-changing style of teaching have been committed to professionally produced one-hour tapes. They are regularly used by schools, churches and small groups.

T-Shirts

Attractive T-shirts and sweatshirts display the condensed message of each book.

Newsletter

Gayle Erwin publishes a popular, informative newsletter called **Servant Quarters**. Sent free in the USA.